Score Reading

Score Reading

A KEY TO THE MUSIC EXPERIENCE

Michael Dickreiter

Translated by Reinhard G. Pauly

AMADEUS PRESS
Portland, Oregon

Reprinted 2001

Printed in Hong Kong

Amadeus Press
The Haseltine Building
133 S.W. Second Avenue, Suite 450
Portland, Oregon 97204, U.S.A.

Library of Congress Cataloging-in-Publication Data

Dickreiter, Michael.
    [Partiturlesen. English]
    Score reading : a key to the music experience / Michael Dickreiter;
translated by Reinhard G. Pauly.
        p.   cm.
    ISBN 1-57467-056-5 (pbk.)
    1. Score reading and playing. I. Title.

MT85.D4713   2000
781.4′23—dc21
                                       00-029319

Contents

1 *Introduction*

Are notes, written or printed, really music? A score represents an arrangement of all components of a composition: all orchestra parts, all vocal solo and choral parts. Does such a score merely indicate what every musician is supposed to sing or play, or is it, in itself, music?

It is a fact that most composers write their music without the help of an instrument, and that many musicians, professionals and competent amateurs, can obtain a clear notion of what a piece sounds like merely by reading the score. They can create for themselves an impression of the sound that does not really exist acoustically.

When we hear music, we do not experience it as variations in air pressure reaching our ears; rather, the physical vibrations are transformed through the brain to become "music." Reading a score can also be a way of experiencing music, but experiencing music by way of its written form, its notation, and by way of its acoustical manifestation are very different. We have a physical and mental (emotional) reaction to music. Certain harmonies please us; certain melodies evoke memories; some sounds, such as a violin tremolo, may send shivers up our spine. Only music that is actually heard is likely to affect us in such ways. Reading music, though, can be compared to studying a menu or reading the description of a landscape: it may stimulate our appetite or our imagination, but only the actual repast or physically seeing the landscape will provide the full enjoyment.

To be sure, the reasons for learning how to read a score are very practical, for both professional and amateur musicians. It is an essential skill for the conductor who has to direct a performance and who is responsible for its overall success. But developing score-reading skills has another important purpose, important especially for readers of this book. Many listeners derive great pleasure from following a performance with score in hand—in the concert hall or opera house, whether broadcast or recorded. European opera houses equip some seats with small reading lamps, to make following a score possible.

What then is to be accomplished by simultaneous reading and listening?

- This kind of score reading provides insights into the musical structure of a work—both the overall design and the details—that are difficult to gain by merely listening, especially during a first listening. "Seeing" the structure facilitates a listener's comprehension of the use of specific instruments and of the relationships between the primary and secondary musical lines or voices.
- Following the score enables us to determine whether the performance is accurate. This, of course, assumes we are using a score that is accurate, one based on the most reliable sources. These in turn may be based on the composer's own handwriting, on the work's first edition, or on a score that was prepared under the composer's supervision. Many editions of music deviate far from these reliable sources, containing changes made later by others. A good printed edition should include information about the sources on which it is based.
- Following a score also makes it possible to identify specific places in it, which is important in a rehearsal or when analyzing a work. When making recordings or supervising broadcasts and telecasts, the engineer or sound director must be able to refer aloud to a specific place, for instance, "the woodwind entrance in measure 320."
- Score reading also enables a recording engineer to anticipate dynamic changes such as a sudden *fortissimo* entrance.

All these aspects of studying a score are important for listeners, not only for conductors and sound directors. The acquired knowledge helps the listener gain an impression of the music's general character; it clarifies the orchestra's exact makeup, the composition's style and form, the prominence of the orchestra's several sections and dynamic levels, and much more.

Compared to studying a score by reading it, playing it on the piano is a more challenging task requiring advanced pianistic skills and much practice. The person who is chiefly interested in following a score while listening need only know the general principles involved. The pianist must understand the notation of every instrument and must read not only the standard clefs but also some rarely used ones. A pianist is additionally challenged to reproduce on the piano the varied timbres, or tone colors, of orchestral sound.

This book's objective is to provide the knowledge required for following a score while listening and, before listening, to obtain from the score all necessary information about the orchestra's makeup and the music's general formal arrangement. Acquiring this knowledge may also serve as preparation for studying a score without actually listening—the way a reader might examine a poem and its form without actually hearing it recited.

The one desirable prerequisite for our study is a fairly good reading knowledge of music notation. If this demand discourages you, I should add that it is often sufficient to be able to follow the notation of a single musical line. To "sightread" music with ease is not necessary, nor is the knowledge of every notational symbol. If, at the beginning, your knowledge of music theory is modest, your interest in the subject is likely to grow with the continued study of scores. One further desirable skill is the ability to recognize the most important musical instruments by their sound.

This book will inform you about various types of scores and their uses, about their historical development, about the visual appearance of various kinds of notation, about techniques of following a score, and about orchestras and their conductors. It then gives first exercises in score reading. Chapter 6 contains practice examples taken from scores of different style periods and arranged in order of increasing difficulty. Well-known works were selected because you may own recordings of them or will be able to find them easily. To develop facility in score reading continued practice is essential, just as it is for learning to play an instrument.

2 Types of Scores

A score is a systematic arrangement of all parts of a composition, both vocal and instrumental. The Italian word for score is *partitura*, meaning "division" or "arrangement." The individual parts are arranged on the page in such a way that tones heard simultaneously are notated exactly above and below each other. Vertical dividing lines going through all or most parts are the most obvious aspect of this arrangement; they facilitate the precise alignment of simultaneously sounding tones. Bar lines later developed from these lines.

Today we distinguish among various types of scores according to function. These types include simplified versions that do not reproduce all voices or instruments but are easier to read and more useful for certain purposes.

For rehearsing and performing a conductor uses a full score. This is the standard score and usually the first one printed. It came to be called "full" to distinguish it from a "study score" printed in a smaller format. The large size of a full score leaves room on the paper for notations by the conductor. The large print also accommodates the greater distance from the conductor's eyes to the score lying on the music stand—greater than that of a hand-held score read from a sitting position.

Study scores, also called pocket scores, are widely used today. Their smaller size makes them more convenient and less expensive to produce; therefore, they have become popular with students and amateurs (see figure 1). A study or pocket score is as complete as a conductor's full score; it is produced by a photo-mechanical reduction in size. Small-sized scores already existed in the early nineteenth century, as shown by early editions of some Beethoven symphonies, but the publishing of pocket scores became widespread around 1900. Ernst

Eulenburg in Leipzig was an early publisher. Since then, small-sized scores of piano and chamber music have also become popular.

1. Relative sizes of full score and study score (Beethoven, Fifth Symphony)

Before the time of recordings, most music, especially operas and symphonies, was studied at the piano. For this purpose, publishers provided piano reductions or vocal scores, for operas, oratorios, and so on. These reduced scores continue to be used today for study and rehearsal purposes.

Full scores also exist for electronic music, but their appearance is radically different from traditional scores. They consist chiefly of technical instructions concerning the various sound generators. Such scores are rarely suitable for following the music, and they are seldom published in quantity. (One reason for publishing is to establish copyright.) Simplified scores using some traditional symbols occasionally are issued after the work has been produced.

Attempts have been made to reduce the difficulty of score reading for untrained listeners. Some scores contain only the parts for a small group of singers or players within a large ensemble; the other parts appear either in a piano reduction or are omitted altogether. Such scores may show only the vocal parts of a work for soloists, chorus, and orchestra. To facilitate following a composition, publishers have experimented with "melodic line scores" in which only the line that is most prominent at a given point is printed. Such reductions, to be sure, can no longer be considered scores and hardly help in developing score-reading skill.

Piano scores and vocal scores became increasingly important in the nineteenth century as the piano was perfected and ever more widely used. A piano score is a reduction of an orchestral score, including all its essential parts or lines. Often the names of instruments prominent at a given moment are printed above the music. If a large orchestral score is condensed this way, playing it requires great pianistic skill, though an experienced pianist can simplify the task by quickly seeing which notes can be left out. If a work includes solo or choral singing, those parts usually are printed in their entirety above the piano reduction, which then becomes a vocal or piano-vocal score. Vocal scores are widely used, but printed piano reductions of orchestral works are rare today. Instrumental solo concertos are commonly available in editions giving the complete solo part plus a piano reduction of the orchestral accompaniment. Such an edition of a violin concerto would be called an edition for violin and piano.

Today vocal scores are essential for rehearsing major works for solo voices, chorus, and orchestra. It is to a singer's advantage to be able to follow the entire work, even while he or she has an extended rest. Figure 2 compares a measure from J. S. Bach's *St. John Passion* as it appears in a full score and in a vocal score. The full score includes first and second oboe, first and second violin, and viola. Then, at the bottom of the page, are organ and continuo, the latter here consisting of cello, string bass, and bassoon. In the vocal score these parts are condensed in such a way that the pianist's ten fingers can reproduce them all. The words "Violins (without flutes)" refer to the full scoring,

2. Full score (top) and vocal score (bottom) (J. S. Bach, *St. John Passion*)

meaning that in an earlier, similar passage two flutes doubled the violin parts. Here the pianist would play the first violin part with the right hand, the bass line (organ, second violin, and viola) with the left hand.

Major symphonic works also were published in arrangements for four-hand piano. Original keyboard music for two players already existed in Mozart's time, and an 1845 picture by Adolph von Menzel shows his daughter and son seated at the piano, playing four-hand music (see figure 3).

3. *Adolph von Menzel: The Artist and His Family* (1845)

Piano and vocal scores were first issued around 1750, but it was not until about 1830 that lithographic printing methods made it possible to market large printruns and reduce the price of a score. Some famous composers, especially Liszt, prepared piano scores (and free arrangements) of works by other composers. But today's music lovers are more likely to familiarize themselves with a composition by listening to a recording while following a full score or pocket score rather than a piano score.

3 *The Look of a Score*

Parts, lines, brackets

Most orchestra instruments are melody instruments whose parts are notated on a single line or staff. String instruments, although basically melody instruments, can also play chords and occasionally do so in orchestral music. But even a violin part that includes chords is notated on one staff. Instruments that require two lines or staves are the celesta, harp, piano, and xylophone, among others.

To save space on the score page and improve legibility, the parts of two or more instruments sometimes are written on one staff. Publishers usually combine two similar wind parts, such as two flutes or two oboes, but rarely two string parts. If the parts for two instruments share one staff, and at one point they play the same notes, the notes will have two stems, up and down, or carry the notation "a 2."

In orchestral music, each string part is played by several players, whereas each wind part has only one player. Thus a small orchestra may have six first violins, all playing the same music; a large symphony orchestra may have sixteen or, rarely, as many as twenty-four. Sometimes a string part, such as a violin part, may be divided so the players at the first stand have different notes from those at the second stand, or the two players at one stand have different notes. This is indicated by the Italian word *divisi*.

Brackets or braces at the beginning of a score page indicate which instruments belong together. Brackets (see figure 4) identify the woodwind, brass, and string groups. Within the brass bracket, braces set off the four horns, three trumpets, and three trombones. Braces group together the two staves of a piano or harp part. Braces may also group the cello and bass parts; before 1800 they often played identical notes, and even later their parts tended to be similar. In older printed scores, a bar line was drawn from top to bottom through all parts. Today, for greater clarity, the lines go only through groups of instruments that belong together. In figure 4 the line extends through all winds, then breaks to form a separate bar line for the harp and another for the

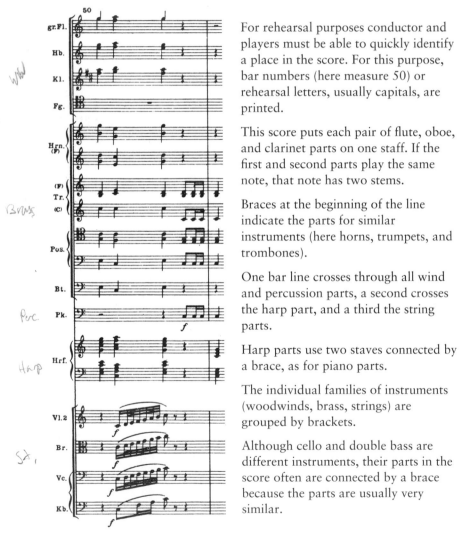

For rehearsal purposes conductor and players must be able to quickly identify a place in the score. For this purpose, bar numbers (here measure 50) or rehearsal letters, usually capitals, are printed.

This score puts each pair of flute, oboe, and clarinet parts on one staff. If the first and second parts play the same note, that note has two stems.

Braces at the beginning of the line indicate the parts for similar instruments (here horns, trumpets, and trombones).

One bar line crosses through all wind and percussion parts, a second crosses the harp part, and a third the string parts.

Harp parts use two staves connected by a brace, as for piano parts.

The individual families of instruments (woodwinds, brass, strings) are grouped by brackets.

Although cello and double bass are different instruments, their parts in the score often are connected by a brace because the parts are usually very similar.

4. Parts, brackets, and braces (Wagner, Prelude to *Die Meistersinger von Nürnberg*)

strings. If, as in figure 5, more than one score page is printed on one page, they are separated by two short diagonal lines.

Remember here, and throughout the book, that one rigid, uniform system of organizing a score page does not exist. Only general conventions have evolved over time. Music publishers, at various times and places, have developed their own systems, and new developments

The direction "div." means *divisi*; for this tremolo, half the violins play the upper, the other half the lower note.

Two short diagonal lines help to separate two systems on one score page.

The rehearsal letter "O" appears here, as explained in Figure 4.

The word "Tutti" shows that from here on all second violins play; only half the section played before.

Here, the viola part is not divided. One player can play both notes, performing a "double stop."

5. Instruments; additional instructions to players (Richard Strauss, *Don Juan*)

in vocal and instrumental music have brought about new approaches to score notation, as they may in the future.

How to determine a score's makeup or instrumentation

Among the first questions a reader will ask is: what instruments are playing in this piece? A list of all the included instruments would be helpful at the beginning of a composition, just as the dramatis personae at the beginning of a play. But such a list is rare in orchestral scores, perhaps because compositions such as traditional symphonies use a fairly standard lineup of instruments. In the absence of a list at the beginning, look on the first page of music for the exact instrumentation. There instruments may be listed even if they are not heard right away; in that case the staff in question will have measures of rests. After the first score page, to save space, subsequent pages will print only those parts that play at the time. Therefore, if the first page shows parts with rests only, that page almost certainly indicates the work's complete instrumentation (see figure 6). Not evident at this point, however, is the possibility that later in the work a player may exchange instruments. Often a flute player will "double" on piccolo or an oboist will double on English horn. Doubling is apparent in a score only at the place of the switch and therefore requires careful reading.

Many compositions have several movements, self-contained parts of the work having their own key and structure. In a performance, movements usually are separated by pauses. All movements of a symphony do not necessarily have the same instrumentation. During the time of Mozart and Beethoven, for instance, trumpets and timpani customarily rested during slow movements. In Beethoven's famous Fifth Symphony the slow movement's scoring is not reduced, but in the last movement it is augmented: piccolo, contrabassoon, and three trombones are added. Thus you will need to ascertain the instrumentation for each movement, but most often the first movement features all instruments. Additions, if any, are likely only in the last movement; many composers bring in all the instruments—"pull out all the stops" —for an effective ending (see figure 7).

Italian has often been called the international language of music, and indeed much of the terminology we use is Italian. During the seventeenth and eighteenth centuries especially, Italian musicians domi-

6. First page of score, giving complete instrumentation (Weber, Overture to *Der Freischütz*)

nated the European musical scene. Since this period also saw the development of score notation, Italian terms became generally accepted, not only for instruments but also for indications of tempo (itself an Italian word!), dynamics, and other expression marks. During the age of nineteenth-century nationalism, composers and publishers made efforts to substitute terms from their own country's language. As a result, scores may give instrument names in French, German, English, or occasionally other languages. The table on pages 24–25 gives these names in four languages.

7. First page of score (left) showing only instruments playing at the
beginning; (right) last page showing complete instrumentation (Richard
Strauss, *Till Eulenspiegel*)

At a full score's beginning, also at the beginning of movements, instruments usually are named in full. On subsequent pages they may be abbreviated. If the instrumentation remains the same throughout, names may be omitted altogether; any changes then would be marked above or at the beginning of new lines. The table below gives the most often used abbreviations.

WW

Piccolo: Picc., pte. Fl., kl. Fl.
Flute: Fl., gr. Fl.
Oboe: Ob., Hb., Hautb.
English horn: E. H., C. I., Cor A.
Clarinet: Cl., Kl.
Bass clarinet: Cl. B., B. Kl.
Bassoon: Bssn., Bon., Fg.
Contrabassoon: C. Bssn., C. Bon., C. Fg., K. Fg.

Br

French horn: Hrn., Cor.
Trumpet: Tr.
Trombone: Trb., Ps., Pos.
Tuba: T.b., Tb.

Perc

Timpani: Timp., Timb., Pk.
Bass drum: B. Dr., gr. C., gr. Tr.
Snare drum: C. ch., kl. Tr.
Cymbal: Cymb., Bck., B.

St.

Violin: Vln., Vl., Vn.
Viola: Vla., Va., Vle.
Cello: Vcl., Vc.
Bass: B., Cb., Kb.

Organization of a score page

Instruments are listed and grouped according to certain conventions that go back to the nineteenth century, the age during which professional conductors in the modern sense first appeared. Both earlier and later, deviations from these conventions existed. Sometimes composers used different arrangements of instruments for specific compositions, which show in some modern reprints of older scores.

Figure 8 shows the first page of Schubert's Eighth Symphony, the so-called "Unfinished," which actually is his seventh. The page gives the typical arrangement found in scores from the classic period and beyond. The orchestra is grouped according to families of instruments

Names of Instruments

Italian	English	French	German
Woodwinds			
(flauto) piccolo, ottavino	piccolo, octave flute	piccolo, petite flûte	Piccoloflöte
flauto (grande)	(concert) flute	(grande) flûte	(große) Flöte
flauto contralto	alto flute	flûte alto	Altflöte
flauto dolce	recorder	flûte douce, flûte à bec	Blockflöte
oboe	oboe	hautbois	Oboe
corno inglese	English horn	cor anglais	Englisch Horn
fagotto	bassoon	basson	Fagott
contrafagotto	contrabassoon	contrebasson	Kontrafagott
clarinetto	clarinet	clarinette	Klarinette
corno di bassetto, clarone	basset horn	cor de bassette	Bassetthorn
clarinetto basso	bass clarinet	clarinette basse	Baßklarinette
saxofono soprano	soprano saxophone	saxophone soprano	Sopransaxophon
saxofono contralto	alto saxophone	saxophone alto	Altsaxophon
saxofono tenore	tenor saxophone	saxophone ténor	Tenorsaxophon
saxofono baritono	baritone saxophone	saxophone baryton	Baritonsaxophon
saxofono basso	bass saxophone	saxophone basse	Baßsaxophon
Brass			
tromba	trumpet	trompette	Trompete
corno (a pistoni)	(French) horn	cor (à pistons)	Horn (Ventil-)
trombone	trombone	trombone	Posaune
tuba bassa	bass tuba	tuba	Tuba
Percussion			
timpani	timpani, kettle drums	timbales	Pauken
gran cassa	bass (big) drum	grosse caisse	große Trommel
cassa chiara	snare (small) drum	caisse claire	kleine Trommel
tamburo militare	military (side) drum	tambour (militaire)	Militärtrommel
tamburo provenzale	tabor (drum of Provence)	tambourin (provençal)	Provenzalische Trommel

Italian	English	French	German
tamburo basso	long drum	grand tambour	Rührtrommel

cassettina
    (di legno)
	wood block,
	    Chinese block
		bloc en bois	Holzblock

tam tam	tam-tam	tam-tam	Tamtam
gong	gong	gong	Gong
triangolo	triangle	triangle	Triangel
piatto	cymbal	cymbale	Becken
campana	(steeple) bell	(grande) cloche	Glocke

Instruments struck with beaters

silofono	xylophone	xylophone	Xylophon
campanelli	bells, glockenspiel	jeu de timbres, glockenspiel	Glockenspiel

Plucked instruments

harpa	harp	harpe	Harfe
chitarra	guitar	guitare	Gitarre
liuto	lute	luth	Laute

Keyboard instruments

pianoforte	piano	piano	Klavier
clavicembalo	harpsichord	clavecin	Cembalo
organo	organ	orgue(s)	Orgel
celesta	celesta	célesta	Celesta

Strings

violino	violin	violon	Violine
viola	viola	alto	Viola, Bratsche
violoncello	violoncello	violoncelle	Violoncello
contrabasso, basso, violone	double bass	contrebasse	Kontrabaß

8. Arrangement of instruments on the score page for a medium-sized orchestra (Schubert, Eighth Symphony)

based on manner of tone production, generally woodwinds, brass, percussion, and strings. The groups are identified by brackets. Percussion instruments are below the brass. Within a group, an instrument's range determines its place, from high to low. French horns are an exception. According to their range they should fall between trumpets and trombones, but their notation traditionally appears above the other brass instruments. Their tone quality (timbre) blends especially well with that of the woodwinds, and composers often use horns and woodwinds together. The organization of a score page outlined below has been the standard from the mid-eighteenth century on.

Woodwinds:	Flutes
	Oboes
	Clarinets
	Bassoons
Brass:	Horns
	Trumpets
	Trombones
Percussion:	Timpani
	Other percussion
Strings:	Violins
	Violas
	Cellos
	Basses

During the nineteenth century composers increased the orchestra's tonal palette by adding more wind instruments, though the typical scoring continued to be used, as in the Schubert score in figure 8. Additional woodwind instruments are played by musicians who usually play another instrument in the same family. Thus the English horn is played by an oboist. A nineteenth-century addition to the brass family is the tuba. On the score page, additional wind instruments appear above or below the one to which they are related, depending on their range. The piccolo part is printed above the flute, the English horn below the oboe, the small (E-flat) clarinet above the normal (B-flat or A) clarinet, the bass clarinet below the others, the contrabassoon below the bassoon. According to this scheme, the wind instruments in a large orchestral score will appear on the page in the order below.

Woodwinds:	Piccolo
	Flutes
	Oboes
	English horn
	Small (E-flat) clarinet
	Clarinets
	Bass clarinet
	Bassoons
	Contrabassoon

Brass: Horns
              Trumpets
              Trombones
              Tuba

Among the percussion instruments, timpani (kettle drums) are listed on top because they are tuned to specific pitches and provide more than rhythm. To some extent, especially during the baroque period, they functioned as bass instruments, playing the rhythm patterns also heard from the trumpets. Below the timpani, other percussion instruments, those with indefinite pitch, are scored, such as triangle, cymbals, and various drums.

Only one plucked instrument has become a member of the standard symphony orchestra: the harp. Its place on the page is between the percussion group and the first violin.

Saxophones are rarely heard in classic orchestral music. When they are included, their parts appear below either woodwinds or brass. Equally rare is the organ; it would be scored below the string basses.

For concertos with orchestral accompaniment, the solo part is printed above the first violin. For large compositions with vocal soloists and chorus (oratorios, Masses, some symphonies, operas), two systems exist. In one, the vocal parts, soloists above chorus, are placed between viola and cello. This is an old custom, going back to baroque operas and oratorios, where voices and the instrumental bass formed a work's nucleus. The tradition still applies to Mozart's *Requiem* (1791; see figure 9a) and to many works throughout the nineteenth century. The other system places the voice parts above the first violins, as in Beethoven's Ninth Symphony (1822–1824; see figure 9b).

In choral music, four-part writing (soprano, alto, tenor, bass, abbreviated SATB) is the norm. These four parts are also the standard solo voices, plus mezzosoprano and baritone (high bass voice). A score that merely indicates SATB can mean soloists or chorus. Most scores will carry the direction *tutti*, meaning "all," which calls for chorus (figure 9a), or *soli*, which refers to soloists (figure 9b).

Once again remember that the organization and arrangement of a score page are not rigid, and deviations from the norm are frequent. Wagner, for instance, lists wind instruments strictly according to their range or register, so the English horn part is printed below the clarinet,

9. Placement of vocal parts on the score page: (a) above the cello part (Mozart, *Requiem*); (b) above the first violin (Beethoven, Ninth Symphony)

and the bass clarinet below the bassoon. In some cases valid musical reasons call for deviations, but sometimes new editions of older scores change an unusual arrangement to conform to the norm. Figure 10 shows how the score of a very large late romantic composition, with soloists and chorus, might be organized.

Scores for smaller, so-called chamber orchestras again use two systems—either the parts are listed according to their range, or the familiar grouping found in larger orchestral works is adopted. Figure 11a shows the beginning of J. S. Bach's Brandenburg Concerto No. 2. The highest instrument is the trumpet; it appears above the three other solo

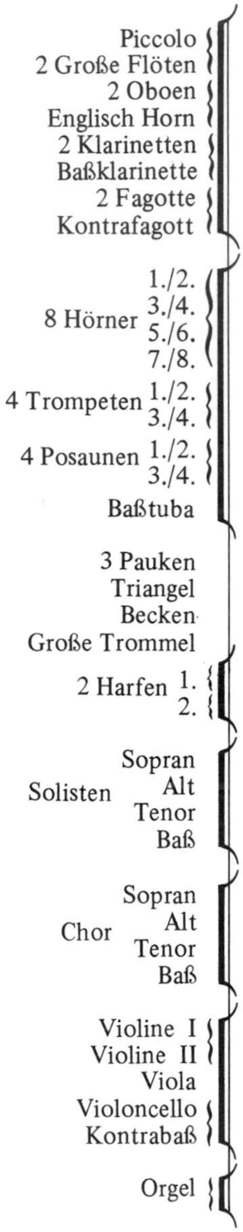

Piccolo
2 Große Flöten
2 Oboen
Englisch Horn
2 Klarinetten
Baßklarinette
2 Fagotte
Kontrafagott

8 Hörner 1./2.
3./4.
5./6.
7./8.

4 Trompeten 1./2.
3./4.

4 Posaunen 1./2.
3./4.

Baßtuba

3 Pauken
Triangel
Becken
Große Trommel

2 Harfen 1.
2.

Solisten Sopran
Alt
Tenor
Baß

Chor Sopran
Alt
Tenor
Baß

Violine I
Violine II
Viola
Violoncello
Kontrabaß

Orgel

10. Large score with vocal soloists and chorus

instruments; together, the four form the *concertino*, the group of solo instruments. Due to its construction, the baroque trumpet has a slim sound that blends well with the other three solo instruments, even with the recorder that appears below the trumpet. In J. S. Bach's day the word *flauto*, used by itself, meant the recorder. Our modern flute was called *flauto traverso*. Under the recorder part appear the oboe and violin, and below the concertino appears the small string orchestra, the *ripieno*, a term that indicates several players on each part. Figure 11b shows a chamber music score in which the arrangement on the page corresponds to that of an orchestral score. The three braces set off woodwinds, horn, and strings. Figure 11c represents a chamber music work with piano. In works of this kind the piano part always is at the bottom of the score; above it, the other parts are placed according to the two practices described.

Notation of individual instruments

The parts of most orchestra instruments are written in the G clef, also called the violin or treble clef, some in the F, or bass clef. Alto and tenor clefs are used for a few instruments. The lists below give the major orchestra instruments and their usual notation, but here, too, exceptions occur, for some composers or for specific works. The most important instruments using the G clef are

> Violin
> Flute (including piccolo, alto flute, recorder)
> Oboe (including English horn)
> Clarinet (including alto clarinet, basset horn,
>   bass clarinet)
> Saxophone (soprano, alto, tenor, baritone,
>   bass saxophones)
> French horn
> Trumpet

A few of the above are tenor or bass instruments, namely alto clarinet, basset horn, bass clarinet; tenor, baritone, and bass saxophones; and the low-pitched horns. The notation for these and some other instruments is a "finger notation," meaning the written note indicates the fingering rather than the pitch. Such instruments are called trans-

11. Various chamber music score arrangements: (a) according to range (J. S. Bach, Brandenburg Concerto No. 2); (b) as in an orchestral score (Schubert, Octet); (c) chamber work with piano (Schubert, "The Trout" Quintet)

posing instruments—a concept that at first is somewhat confusing. We shall come back to it soon.

The following parts are written in the bass clef:

Cello
String bass (double bass)
Bassoon and contrabassoon
Bass trombone
Tuba

Bass clarinet and French horn parts sometimes are written in the bass clef, but G clef is more customary.

Only two instruments consistently employ the alto clef:

Viola
Alto trombone

The tenor clef is used for

Tenor trombone
Cello (occasionally)
Bassoon (occasionally)

The notation of percussion instruments has been less standardized. Instruments with indefinite pitch include drums, cymbals, triangle, tam tam, and many others. In older scores their parts were written on five-line staves, using bass or G clef, or sometimes no clef. More recently, their parts have been written on a single line. Quite often the parts of several percussion instruments are written on one staff or around a single line.

Timpani parts are written on a five-line staff, bass clef, with no key signature. Their tuning is indicated at the beginning, before the five-line staff or above it, for instance, "Timpani in A and E." Before 1800, timpani parts were written in C, regardless of the composition's key. They were treated as transposing instruments, so that "C" always meant the key note or tonic, and "G" the fifth scale step or dominant.

Parts for percussion instruments with definite pitch (such as the timpani) may be written in the G clef or bass clef. To this group also belong marimba, xylomarimba, xylophone, vibraphone, glockenspiel, gong, tubular bells, and others. They sound as written—they are not transposing instruments—except that a few sound one or rarely two octaves higher than written. No uniform notation system exists for this large group.

Transposing instruments

Today's orchestra includes wind instruments built in several different keys, the result of a time when brass instruments did not yet have valves and therefore could not produce complete scales and all half steps. Woodwind instruments also were limited, having only primitive key mechanisms. French horns (the earlier hunting horns) were built in various keys. In a symphony movement in C major, for instance, the players used horns built in that key; in a composition in E major, E-horns were required. A player might have to change instruments within a composition, sometimes within one movement of a symphony.

In the nineteenth century the mechanisms of many wind instruments were greatly improved, but these instruments still are built in different keys because they have different ranges and timbres. A clarinetist therefore has to play on instruments of different size; most often they are built in the keys of B-flat and A, also in C and E-flat. They differ in length, but the system of covering the holes (with fingers, keys, rollers) is largely the same.

Because the clarinets vary in length, the same fingering will produce a different tone on different instruments. In order to produce the same tone on different clarinets, the player would have to learn different fingerings. To avoid this, the written music does not show the actual *sound* wanted but the *fingering* needed to produce that sound. The rationale is that the same written note in any clarinet part will cause the player to use the same fingering, but the actual tone will be different depending on what clarinet is played. To repeat: clarinet notation is a finger notation, not a pitch notation. The clarinet and other instruments with this discrepancy are called transposing instruments. Most transposing instruments are wind instruments.

The following table shows the actual tones produced on various clarinets if they play the written note C:

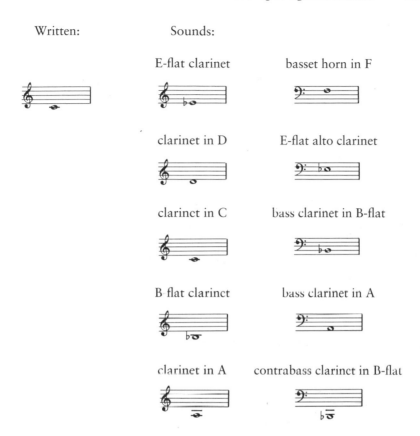

Written: Sounds:

To identify transposing instruments in a score is easy. The beginning of the line in question will not merely say "clarinet" or "trumpet," but "clarinet in A," "trumpet in B-flat," "horn in F," and so on. Thus the label "clarinet in E-flat" indicates that the written note C will sound E-flat. Unfortunately, the label "in F" does not indicate to which octave to transpose, up or down—knowing the instrument in question and its range is the only way to discern the appropriate octave.

To discuss all possible transpositions would go beyond the scope of this book. Instead, here are the two most frequently encountered cases: clarinet in B-flat and horn in F. First, the B-flat clarinet, the principles of which also apply to B-flat trumpet, B-flat horn, and other instruments in that key. In the following figures, the written notes and sounding tones are vertically aligned. If a C major scale is played, a B-flat major scale will sound, a whole tone lower:

Written:

Sounds

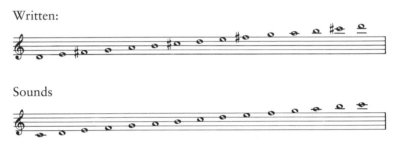

Conversely, if a C major scale is expected to sound, a D major scale—a whole tone higher—must be written:

Written:

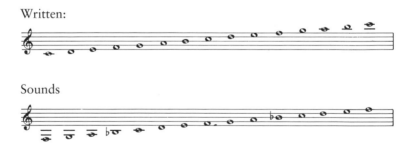

Sounds

How does this work for instruments in another key? For the English horn and the French horn, both in F, each note sounds a fifth lower than written. Both instruments use the G clef:

Written:

Sounds

The instruments that sound an octave higher or lower than written, strictly speaking, also are transposing instruments. The string bass part is written in the bass clef; it sounds an octave lower than written. The same is true of the contrabassoon:

Written:    Sounds

Piccolo, soprano recorder, and celesta are written in the G clef and sound an octave higher than written:

Guitar music is written in the G clef and sounds an octave lower than written. Music for the tenor voice is also transposed an octave down. In modern choral scores the tenor part is often written, correctly, in the "octave G clef" 𝄞 :

One way to recognize transposing instruments in a score (unless they transpose by an octave) is by their different key signature—different, for instance, from the strings. If the strings play in C major, the B-flat clarinet part will have the key signature of D major, the English horn of G major. The parts will have two sharps or one sharp respectively at the beginning of their lines. The situation is different for trumpets and French horns, whether or not they are transposing. For them, the necessary accidentals appear directly in front of the note in question—no key signature is at the beginning of the line. At first glance therefore it seems as though trumpet and horn parts are always written in C major or A minor. Timpani parts also are written without key signature, but the tuning is indicated at the beginning. (Usually an orchestra has two or three kettle drums.)

Historical reasons account for the fact that French horn and trumpet parts are written without key signature. In the eighteenth (and, in the case of the horns, still in much of the nineteenth) century, so-called natural instruments were used. Trumpets of that age might be compared to bugles: they cannot play all steps of the scale but only the natural tones, based on the overtone series. Horns and trumpets therefore had to be built in many keys. A composition in F major required horns and trumpets in F. In that case, no key signature and no notes with accidentals (sharps or flats) were required. During the nineteenth century, valve horns and trumpets took the place of the natural ones. They can play all whole steps and half steps, but the old manner of notation has persisted. Even today scores and parts are printed as though the valves had not been invented. The French horn currently used is the F horn, or the double horn in F and B-flat. Horn players use these even when the score calls for a horn in E, or D, or any other key. Players are challenged to make the transpositions required, but most have become so used to this custom that they oppose a simplification of the notation. Trumpeters play instruments in B-flat or C regardless of the tuning called for in the score. This adherence to custom is a good example of how strongly ingrained some musical conventions are, resulting in this case in notational practices that are illogical from today's viewpoint.

Here, once more, is an overview of the most important orchestra instruments, indicating whether or at what interval they transpose.

Instrument	Transposing	Sounding note (. . . than written)
Piccolo		one octave higher
Flute	no	
Oboe	no	
English horn		a fifth lower
Clarinet in B-flat		a whole step lower
Bassoon	no	
Contrabassoon		one octave lower
French horn in F		a fifth lower
Trumpet in B-flat		a whole step lower
Trombone	no	
Tuba	no	
Violin	no	
Viola	no	
Cello	no	
Double bass		one octave lower

For following a score while listening you do not need to know precisely how to translate the notation of transposing instruments into the actual sounds. To follow a transposed line, seemingly in a different key, is not likely to bother the listener who does not have absolute, or perfect, pitch; few people, including musicians, have it. It is more important that the reader-listener recognize the up-and-down motion of the line, the melody. But the person who wants to play a score on the piano must be thoroughly familiar with the transposition of each instrument.

That transposed parts continue to take a place in modern scores is due to the tradition discussed above; no urgent, logical reason warrants continuing the practice today. Printing the parts in question with their transposition would suffice. In the early twentieth century, Schoenberg and other composers of twelve-tone music frequently did away with writing transposing parts. In the late twentieth century efforts were made to adopt a so-called reform score in which all parts are notated at actual pitch, known as concert pitch. This type of score certainly would be a boon to those who merely want to follow a score, but conductors and good rehearsal pianists have few problems with the transposing-instrument parts in the scores they use. Moreover, it can be an advantage at rehearsals for conductors and players to look at identical music.

Title pages: "Opus" and other work-numbering systems

On a score's title page, and usually also above the first line of music, some or all of the following information will be listed:

Type of work (symphony, concerto)
Number within that category
Its scoring
Key and mode (major, minor)
Opus number, or number in an established catalog
Composer's name, often with birth and death dates
Further details, such as year of composition, year of first
     performance, name of editor, arranger, and so on

In place of the type of work, a title may be given, such as that of an opera or ballet. In that case, key and scoring would not be listed.

An opus number clearly identifies the work. The custom of giving opus numbers goes back to the seventeenth century. Such a number is meant to assign a chronological place to a work in the composer's oeuvre, but unfortunately this is not always the case. Both composers and publishers at times have assigned opus numbers arbitrarily so that they do not give a clue about the date of composition. Identical works even have appeared with different opus numbers in different editions. For instance, Schubert's Op. 1 is his famous song "The Erl King," written in 1815. But before that he had composed many other works, some well known today, that carry no opus numbers. Since opus numbers can be unreliable and incomplete, more reliable lists with their own numbering systems have been compiled for many composers. These lists often carry the compiler's name and list individual works by name and number. Some important terms and work lists, with their abbreviations, are the following:

Opus, op.	work
Opus posthumum, op. posth.	work published after the composer's death
BWV	Bachwerkverzeichnis, for the works of J. S. Bach
Deutsch-Verzeichnis, Deutsch-V., DV., D.	for the works of Schubert
Hoboken, Hob.	for the works of Haydn
Köchel-Verzeichnis, Köchel, K. V., KV, K.	for the works of Mozart

Partial scores

A *partitino*, Italian for small or partial score, is a score containing the few parts that are not included in the work's full score. These parts, usually for brass and percussion, may have been added later by the composer. The reason they were not included in the full score is not always clear. Aside from those parts added later, a partial score may be showing the parts *ad libitum*, those for optional inclusion. In modern editions of older works, they are incorporated in the full score.

Partial scores of this kind exist for early editions of Haydn and Mozart symphonies (trumpet and timpani parts) and for Beethoven's Ninth Symphony (percussion parts). In Verdi opera scores, all stage music (played onstage or backstage) is printed as a condensed piano score, but more completely as a separate small score. Such stage music, called *banda*, is conducted by an assistant who for this purpose does not need the full score.

4 Scores and Their History

The score's function as something to be studied, by amateurs as well as professional musicians, is a fairly recent one, as is the score's function as an object of scholarly study, to be used for musical analysis. It acquired this use through the emergence of musicology in the nineteenth century. At all times, however, scores have been used chiefly for composing, rehearsing, and performing.

This chapter traces the origin of the score as the composer's medium for writing down a work and follows its evolution to the present day. Its changes are closely related to the orchestra's steady growth, to the increasing number and variety of instruments, to their changing functions, and to the changing ways of writing down their parts. The term *score* not only refers to the sum of vocal and instrumental parts but, in a symbolic way, to the composition itself.

The score's function of enabling a conductor to lead an orchestra in rehearsal and performance will be taken up in chapter 7, along with descriptions of various seating arrangements. These matters became increasingly important during the nineteenth century when orchestras became larger and their music more complex. Before that time conductors as we know them were rare, and scores were not always used in rehearsing and performing.

The first scores

It would be difficult to compose polyphonic music (music having two or more parts) without writing it down in a way that shows the relation of the parts to each other. Few musicians are able to put together (compose) a polyphonic piece entirely in their heads, without putting the

41

parts on paper to show how they fit together—in other words, without a score. A few famous musicians such as J. S. Bach are said to have had that ability; they are the exceptions to the rule.

Historically, even the very first attempts at writing down polyphony represent a kind of score. These documents, dating from the ninth century, are notated in such a way that simultaneous sounds are vertically aligned. Some later medieval manuscripts also have such scorelike arrangements of the voices. In some cases the interpretation is unequivocal; other documents present problems in understanding how to sing the music.

Polyphonic music became ever more widespread during the fifteenth and sixteenth centuries, in fact, the sixteenth century has been called "The Golden Age of Polyphony." Polyphony by that time had become extremely complex and was governed by strict rules of voice leading; composing such music without writing it down in score form is unthinkable. We would therefore assume that many scores would have been preserved in old libraries, but hardly any scores have come down to us. Instead, the music is saved in choir books and part books.

In a typical choir book the individual voice parts, often four, are written on a large double page. On top of the left page is the discant (soprano) part, underneath it the tenor. On the right page is the alto and below it the bass part. In part books, each voice part is written or printed as a separate book. In a sense, the part book arrangement is the form of today's orchestral music: every player has only his or her own music. Singing from a choir book meant that everyone looked at the same page spread; it therefore had to be large (see figure 12a).

Large choir books, handwritten and often beautifully decorated or illuminated, were still used in the seventeenth century; a few exist from as late as the nineteenth century. Part books became widely available in the sixteenth century when music printing was perfected. While choir books served mostly for church singing and for teaching, part books were popular for social music making. Many illustrations of the time show singers and players seated around a table with part books in front of them (see figure 12b).

But where are the scores from these early periods? Composers then worked on plates made of wood or slate on which music staves and vertical lines (resembling our bar lines) had been previously engraved. Once a composition had been scored in this manner, its parts would be

12. (a) The cantor teaches a hymn to the congregation, using a choir book; (b) four musicians sing from part books

transferred to a choir book or to part books. After that, the wooden plate or slate would be erased and could be used again. Such an erasable slate was called a *tabula compositoria*. A few teaching manuals of the time mention them, but the scores have not been preserved. Figure 13a shows such a ten-line tabula. Score sketches on paper (figure 13b) were rarely used and only a few exist today.

Scores for use in performance were first prepared by organists who wanted to play the voice parts of choral compositions on their instrument. These are called keyboard scores or intabulations. While modern keyboard or vocal scores represent condensations for playing on the piano, the earlier keyboard scores were true scores. The first printed ones came from Italy, the earliest dated 1577. Figure 14 shows a keyboard score from 1603. Four parts appear one below another; the vertical lines, roughly corresponding to our bar lines, indicate the alignment which at this time was not yet precise. Titles of some early printed

I II III IIII V VI VII VIII

Hæc eſt ſimplex concordantiarum
compoſitio ſecundum prædictas regu-
las, poſſet enim multo ſubtilius & velo-
tius conſtrui, hoc modo.

Sequitur Reſolutio.

13. (a) *Tabula compositoria;*
(b) (*facing page*) manuscript score
sketch or draft

editions already contain the root of the word *partitura*, the modern
Italian word for score. (The German word is *Partitur*.) We find titles
such as *Musica . . . partite in caselle* or *Tutti i Madrigali . . . spartiti et
accommodati per sonar d'ogni sorte d'Instrumento perfetto*, where
"partite" and "spartiti" refer to the vertical "ordering" lines. The first
German keyboard score or tablature was Samuel Scheidt's *Tabulatura
nova* of 1624. A century later, J. S. Bach still used such keyboard scores.

Another predecessor of the modern score existed in music for a
solo voice with instrumental accompaniment. We have many six-
teenth-century scores for voice and lute accompaniment in which vertical lines appear. The earliest examples of scores as we define them are
scores of the first operas. An opera score includes all directions needed
for performance. The music of these operas was written in score form,
not only for composing but for performance. Figure 15 shows a five-
voice chorus from the opera *Euridice* by Caccini, published in 1600.
For the choruses Caccini omits the instrumental parts because they
double the voice parts. The instrumental bass part is included whenever
the vocal bass has rests, as in the first three measures of the example.
When soloists are singing, the instrumental parts are given but without
identifying specific instruments. Around 1600, the exact choice of
instruments was largely left to the performers.

In operas, then and now, frequent tempo changes occurred, often related to the text, and the choice of instruments often was determined by what was available. Consequently, full scores were needed for opera direction, whereas church music and instrumental music did not require scores until much later. The parts for Beethoven's first six symphonies were published in 1809, the scores not until 1826. Full scores for other than operatic music were printed along with the appearance of professional conductors early in the nineteenth century.

Since 1800 many works have been published in score form that were previously available only in parts. The demand for scores for study purposes is related to the nineteenth-century emergence of historical musicology. Today, much early music is available in score form.

The rest of this chapter traces the development of orchestral scores from the Renaissance to the late twentieth century. Avant garde music has not been included because such scores, if at all published, are extremely difficult to obtain for study purposes.

The scoring of an orchestral work is governed by several factors, chiefly by the conventions of the composer's era. Every age has its traditions of style, including tone color or timbre, and these traditions affect the number and kinds of instruments used. Wind instruments in particular underwent many technological changes that influenced the

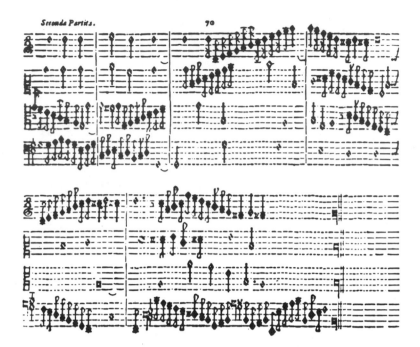

14. Keyboard score (Ascanio Mayone, *Primo libro de diversi capricci per sonare*, Naples 1603)

ways composers wrote for them. Once an orchestra has become standardized, it will affect the way composers write: their works are more likely to be performed if an existing orchestra can play them. Today's standard orchestra in essence is the same as that for which composers wrote 100–150 years ago.

Renaissance and baroque scores

Our modern definition of an orchestra did not yet apply to late renaissance music (ca. 1500–1600), for there were no standardized, widely accepted groups of instruments. Rather, the many different renaissance instruments were combined in a multitude of ways. Availability of voices and instruments determined a group's makeup at a given occasion, with wind instruments being most important. Some instruments, of course, were preferred for certain venues: for outdoor use, for music making in the home, at court, or in church. Loudness or softness of an instrument

15. Opera score (Caccini, "Al canto, al ballo," first chorus from *Euridice*, Florence 1600)

played a part in this. Some instruments traditionally were associated with certain social settings and occasions. Trumpets and timpani accompanied the appearances of kings and high nobility, while flutes (fifes) and drums were played by ordinary foot soldiers. Not until about 1600 did composers pay greater attention to tone color by stipulating specific instruments or combinations of voices and instruments. Early examples can be found in Venetian church music and in early opera.

Around 1600, a new concept of musical style emerged, a style that later came to be called baroque. Polyphonic vocal music had flourished during the sixteenth century, but an important feature of baroque music was the combination of a solo voice accompanied by spare harmonies over a bass line (see figure 16). The required harmonies were indicated by a system of musical shorthand expressed by numbers, or figures, written under the bass line—the so-called figured bass. Harmonies were played on a keyboard instrument (harpsichord or organ) or a plucked instrument that could produce chords (lute or harp), while the bass line was entrusted to a low-pitched string instrument (cello, viola da gamba, string bass) or the bassoon, sometimes both. Depending on the orchestra's size, several chord instruments might play. Chord and bass instruments always belonged together; they were the foundation of baroque music and together constituted the "general bass," in Italian the *basso continuo* or simply *continuo*. Just how the chords indicated by the figures were played or "realized" was up to the player. Many continuo players were so versed in this practice that they did not require any figures; they knew how to realize the bass from the context and the conventions of the time. In a score, basso continuo may be abbreviated as Cont., B. c., or b. c.

16. Figured bass (J. S. Bach, *Christmas Oratorio*)

A baroque orchestra's instrumentation still was less standardized than that of the later classic orchestra. String instruments dominated, with two players to a part, or more depending on local availability. In Italian and German music of the time the string section consisted of first and second violins, viola, and cello, the cello part being doubled by the string bass. This still is the nucleus of today's string section. A baroque orchestra with five string parts, including a second viola, was characteristically French. In either case a chord instrument was added, usually the harpsichord, or in church music the organ.

To this standard string section a few woodwind instruments often were added: two oboes (or two flutes, seldom both) plus a bassoon as an additional bass instrument. A wind trio of two oboes and bassoon was typical for French baroque music—the tradition still affected late eighteenth- and early nineteenth-century symphonies in the trio sections of minuets. Woodwinds were used soloistically (as in J. S. Bach's cantatas and Passions), or they could double violin parts, especially in choral movements. This kind of reinforcing is called *colla parte* writing (see figure 17). For special festive occasions three trumpets (usually in D) were added to the orchestra, normally combined with two kettle drums (timpani). The combination had been traditional even in the Middle Ages and lasted far beyond the baroque era. Since these were natural, valveless trumpets that could only play the overtone series in the key in which they were built, they were restricted to certain melodic patterns and, in the lower register, broken chords.

Figure 18 is an example of a typical late baroque score: one of J. S. Bach's orchestral suites, called overtures, using woodwinds and brass. Trumpets and timpani open the movement; the oboes play *colla parte* most of the time. Trumpets and timpani then rest while the oboes continue the theme. After the repeat, indicated by a double bar, strings

17. *Colla parte* writing (J. S. Bach, Mass in B Minor)

pick up the theme. The continuo instruments are cello, string bass, and bassoon; they "continue" to play while the violins have rests. In this score, the bass is not figured. Trumpet and timpani parts are at the top of the page, as was customary at the time.

Much baroque orchestral music is "concerted," meaning that one or more solo instruments are contrasted with the orchestra. Instruments often featured in solo concertos were violin, flute, oboe, and harpsichord. During solo passages the soloist is accompanied by the group, called *tutti* or *ripieno*; sometimes the continuo is the only

18. Late baroque score (J. S. Bach, Overture No. 4)

accompaniment. During tutti passages, when the orchestra is in the foreground, the soloist plays along, *colla parte*, with the appropriate instrument. In a violin concerto this would be the first violin part. Today many soloists only play their solo sections.

A concerto that features a group of soloists was called a *concerto grosso*, a type also developed in Italy. The solo group, called the *concertino*, is accompanied by the orchestra, also called the tutti, ripieno, or concerto grosso. A string orchestra is the usual accompaniment. The concertino often consists of two violins and a cello (as in figure 19), but many combinations of instruments are found, as for the different concertino in each of J. S. Bach's Brandenburg Concertos.

19. Corelli, Concerto Grosso Op. 6, No. 8, "Christmas Concerto"

Scores of the classic and romantic periods

The years from about 1750 to 1780, following the late baroque era, were an age of transition, variously called preclassic or early classic, to distinguish the time from the classic period that still supplies a large amount of today's concert repertory. Early classic music displays its own style characteristics. The figured bass (continuo) gradually disappears, its function taken over and modified by other instruments. Consistently maintained rhythm patterns—so typical of J. S. Bach—give way to a less driving, *galant* style, often expressing delicate sentiments.

Rhythm, melody, harmony, and timbre all display greater variety. Hand in hand with this variety came an extension of the expressive capabilities of several instruments, and fairly new instruments such as the clarinet became part of the regular orchestra. The string section, however, remained its nucleus, with oboes and horns added as in figure 20, the beginning of Haydn's Cello Concerto in D Major. Here the strings first state the theme; at the beginning of its repetition (the last measure of this example), two oboes and horns reinforce the violins, which results in a different timbre. Later the oboes play independent melodic lines. An important function of the horns is to give fullness to the sound, which they often accomplish with long, sustained notes. During tutti passages the solo cello doubles the appropriate part, here the viola.

The question of whether or not to play a continuo part often arises in music from this period. There is no categorical answer. After 1750 the function of the figured bass was absorbed by the inner voices of the string section, second violin and viola, but in performance the figured bass disappeared only gradually, for the practical reason that performances were directed by the *maestro al cembalo*, the conductor seated at the harpsichord. He would give cues to the players, and especially to any singers, and he generally held the group together, sometimes playing the continuo with one hand only, at other times giving signals by nodding his head. Printed editions seem to have been more conservative with the continuo than the players. Instrumental music was the first to do away with the basso continuo; it disappeared later in opera, and last in church music where as late as 1850 some organ parts used figures. Figured basses are found in many Haydn, Mozart, and Schubert scores. As late as 1856, Bruckner provided figured bass parts in his sacred music. In 1909 Max Reger still (or again?) did the same.

Writers on music have used the terms *classic period* or *Viennese Classicism* for the decades from 1780 to 1830, though today that terminology is no longer universally accepted. Haydn, Mozart, and Beethoven are the best known composers of the age when stylistic trends of the early classic period were developed further. Today's public still regards classic music as one of the high points of music history. It has a certain popular appeal and is easily accessible, often lively, with much melodic, harmonic, and rhythmic contrast and structural clarity. By the classic period, wind instruments had achieved greater importance and melodic prominence, while in early classic music they generally provided accompaniment.

20. Score from the early classic period (Haydn, Cello Concerto in D Major)

Woodwind instruments now tended to be heard as a group that included two each of flutes, oboes, clarinets, and bassoons. Many Mozart symphonies still lack clarinets and flutes, but Haydn's last symphonies consistently call for doubled woodwinds, and Beethoven in some symphonies goes beyond that. This woodwind group has largely remained the standard, not only during the first half of the nineteenth century (Schubert, Schumann, Mendelssohn), but to some extent even in the second half (Bruckner, Brahms, Dvořák, Tchaikovsky, and many others) and for many twentieth-century orchestral works.

Before 1800, the brass consisted of two horns and two trumpets, the latter often rhythmically going with two timpani. After 1800 the group expanded to four horns, two to three trumpets, and three trombones. Wind instruments in general now almost equal the strings in importance. In early classic music orchestras often could omit the wind parts without seriously affecting the work; later, this became out of the question. Figure 21 is an example of a classic score that shows the emancipation of the winds. We will examine these twenty-six measures of Beethoven's "Leonore" Overture No. 3, observing how the various instruments are featured.

The piece begins with a slow introduction, the Adagio, followed by the main section, a lively Allegro. A descending scale in woodwinds and strings sets the mood for the opening. It seems to head towards the key note C, the tonic, but unexpectedly stops at F-sharp, a tone quite foreign to the key of C major. In measures 5–7 bassoons, cellos, and basses interpret the F-sharp harmonically in a way that makes the return to C major possible (m. 8). The strings also are involved in this transition, but unexpectedly they lead to A-flat major (m. 9), a key that stands in a closer relationship to the tonic key than the earlier F-sharp of the bassoons.

In measures 9–13 the woodwinds present a theme, accompanied by the strings. During these measures the trombones substitute for the horns, because the E-flat, required by the harmony, could not be played on the natural horns in C and E. Measures 14–20 bring further modulation, or harmonic change, first in the strings, then with an added flute. This leads to B major, relating harmonically back to measure 7. In retrospect, the wind theme turns out to be an interpolation.

Beginning in measure 20 is a kind of coquettish imitation between first violin and flute, joined in measure 24 by cello and bass. All the winds now contribute to the sense of harmonic forward motion with a tremendous crescendo. A modulation leads back to A-flat major, the key of the wind theme (m. 9–13). Perhaps, then, this theme was an anticipation rather than an interpolation. In the introduction's remaining measures, not printed here, strings and winds alternate and soon reach the Allegro, the main portion of the overture.

This study should clearly show how the early classic orchestra—basically a string orchestra reinforced by a few winds—by Beethoven's time had grown into a body of sound in which clearly differentiated groups have equal importance. Each group at one time or other may lead. This orchestra apparently was considered ideal for music of the West-

21. Score from the later classic period (Beethoven, "Leonore" Overture No. 3) *(continues on pages 56 and 57)*

ern world in general, for it has remained the norm to the present day.

Nevertheless, some further growth took place in the nineteenth century. Some string parts are at times marked *divisi*, which means players of that part, for example, the first violins, do not all play the same music. Cello and bass parts similarly have achieved independence from each other. New wind instruments also appear. With Beethoven, piccolo flute and contrabassoon already had joined the woodwind family. Next the English horn added range and timbre to the oboes, and the

bass clarinet similarly broadened the spectrum of the clarinets. Due to these additions, triple woodwinds were typical for the mid- and later nineteenth century. Comparable changes took place in the brass section: four horns, two or three trumpets, three trombones, and now the tuba. Late nineteenth-century composers such as Wagner, Mahler, and especially Richard Strauss further enlarged the wind section, bringing each woodwind group up to four players. The resulting sound volume

necessitated a correspondingly larger string section. Likewise the number and variety of percussion instruments grew.

Given this large apparatus composers, not surprisingly, also used it selectively, not always writing for all instruments and combinations of instruments that made up the late romantic orchestra. With many deviations from the norm, a "standard" orchestra might best be defined as a statistical average.

A good example of a nineteenth-century score with triple wood-winds is Wagner's Prelude to his opera *Tristan and Isolde* (1865; figure 22). It clearly shows how far both the technical development of instruments and the art of writing for them had progressed. The famous opening theme is first given to the cellos but continued by the wood-winds. Strings and woodwinds have become equals; they produce a blended sound.

Figure 23, an excerpt from Mussorgsky's *Pictures at an Exhibition*

22. A nineteenth-century score (Wagner, Prelude to *Tristan and Isolde*)

23. Contrasting instrumental colors (Mussorgsky, *Pictures at an Exhibition*, arranged by Ravel)

24. Giant orchestras, ca. 1900: (a) Mahler, Second Symphony; (b) Stravinsky, *The Rite of Spring*

as orchestrated by Ravel, demonstrates a different approach to orchestration. The scoring is the same as that for the *Tristan* Prelude except for the percussion section, but while Wagner's work smoothly blends various timbres, Ravel calls for contrasting colors in quick succession.

It would go beyond the scope of this survey to study in detail the development of nineteenth-century orchestration (and hence of score reading), but we can say that two trends emerge after Beethoven. The first remains closely tied to his ideas, shows further development, and occasionally even incorporates elements of baroque style. Mendelssohn, Schumann, and Brahms represent this conservative trend. The second trend is represented by the music of innovators, by the avant garde composers of their time. They may still show ties to Beethoven, for instance to his Sixth Symphony. Berlioz, Liszt, and Wagner are among these innovators, with Bruckner's style fitting somewhere between these trends. With their sometimes gigantic orchestras, Richard Strauss and Mahler reveal how much the art of instrumentation has grown. Other composers, among them Schoenberg and Stravinsky, in essence left the nineteenth century behind, though they too at times resorted to the huge orchestras of the preceding generation. Figure 24 shows two such monster scores: Mahler's Second Symphony (1894) with quadruple woodwinds, and Stravinsky's "Sacrificial Dance" from *The Rite of Spring* (1913; here in the composer's 1947 revision) with quintuple woodwinds. In his *Gurrelieder* (1900–1911) Schoenberg uses even more woodwinds, and the brass section is correspondingly enlarged. Stravinsky's score calls for eight horns, five trumpets, three trombones, and two bass tubas.

The table below shows the overall growth of woodwind and brass sections. The table on pages 62–63 furnishes more detail, based on a few works or groups of works.

Year	Fl.	Ob.	Cl.	Bssn.	Picc.	E. H.	B. Cl.	C. Bssn.	Hrn.	Tr.	Trb.	Tb.
1750–1770		2							2			
1770–1790	1	2		2					2			
after 1790	2	2	2	2					2	2	3	
after 1840	2	2	2	2	1	1	1	1	4	3	3	1
after 1870	3	3	3	3	1	1	1	1	4	3	3	1

Composer and works	Woodwinds					
	Fl.	Ob.	Cl.	Bssn.	Picc.	E. H.
Haydn						
symphonies ca. 1770		2				
ca. 1785	1	2		2		
ca. 1795	2	2	2	2		
Mozart						
symphonies ca. 1770		2				
ca. 1788	1	2		2		
Beethoven						
symphonies 1800–1812	2	2	2	2		
Fifth Symphony (1808)	2	2	2	2	1	
Ninth Symphony (1824)	2	2	2	2	1	
Schubert						
symphonies ca. 1825	2	2	2	2		
Mendelssohn						
Symphony No. 4 (1842)	2	2	2	2		
Schumann						
Symphony No. 4 (1841)	2	2	2	2		
Brahms						
symphonies ca. 1880	2	2	2	2		
Bruckner						
symphonies 1863–1883	2	2	2	2		
Symphony Nos. 8 and 9 ca. 1890	3	3	3	3		
Liszt						
Symphonic poems (1850–1860)	2	2	2	2	1	
Mahler						
Symphony No. 9 (1909)	4	3	3	4	1	1
Schoenberg						
Gurrelieder (1910)	4	3	5	3	4	2

Woodwinds		Brass				Percussion	
B. Cl.	C. Bssn.	Hr.	Tr.	Trb.	Tb.	Timp.	Other Perc.
		2					
		2					
		2	2			x	
		2					
		2	2			x	
		2	2			x	
	1	2	2	3		x	
	1	4	3	3		x	x
		2	2	3		x	x
		4	2			x	
		4	2	3		x	
	1	4	2	3		x	
		4	3	3	1	x	
		8	3	3	1	x	
		4	3	3	1	x	x
1	1	4	3	3	1	x	x
2	2	10	7	7	1	x	x

Orchestras such as these could hardly be exceeded in size. Indeed, twentieth-century groups soon tended to be smaller, though the instrumentation was more varied than that of eighteenth-century orchestras. Even today, the basic orchestra of the classic and romantic periods has remained the standard, with double or triple woodwinds. For the performance of works with many more and unusual instruments, extra players may have to be hired, which puts a strain on the budgets of many performing organizations.

5 Reading a Score—Hearing a Score

To listen to music while following a score, two quite different sensory impressions, reading and hearing, have to be synchronized and compared. Either the aural impressions—hearing music—are transposed into music notation, or the notation—reading music—is transposed into sound. In practice, these two processes may go on simultaneously.

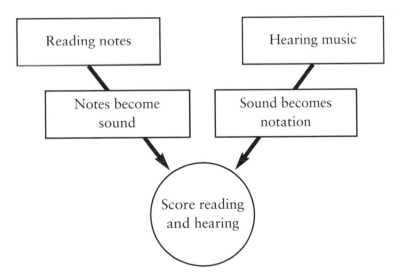

This task presents several ways of approach. Well-trained musicians can read a score "like a newspaper," without thinking much about names of notes, intervals between notes, and the like. As they read the music they arrive at a more or less precise impression of its sound, just as we derive, from reading words in their relation to each other, the meaning of a sentence or paragraph. To read music in this way requires much practice and experience. Active music making, singing and playing, is the best way to acquire this skill.

Let it be said once more, though, for the benefit of those who are less versed in reading music: to *follow* a score it is not absolutely necessary to know the names of all notes and intervals or to recognize all instruments at once by their sound. Nor does one have to be able to read simultaneously all lines on a score page. Not even competent conductors can do this. They can read a few lines at a time, but most importantly they can quickly see what is essential. For our purposes that is more important than following every secondary accompanying part.

Methods for following a score

1.   The first method to practice is picking out one part from the complex web of a score. This part should be prominent and easy to recognize. For beginners, a voice part is most suitable because the text helps in following it. Concertos for a solo instrument and orchestra also are good practice material. In a purely orchestral composition one might follow the first violin part or, in baroque music, the bass line.

2.   A little more challenging would be a work of chamber music, in which the most prominent melodic line may wander from one instrument to another.

3.   Another way to follow a score without losing your place would be to concentrate on the rhythm, to count the accented beats in a measure. This method works in much music from about 1600 to 1900, music in which rhythm is pronounced and regular. Counting works well for following the score of a large, complex, or fast composition, especially for those with little experience in note reading. Counting, even counting out loud, may be the surest way to avoid getting lost. It also helps with following less clearly audible parts.

4.   Another method for following a score, for keeping your place or finding it again, is to be on the lookout for places in the music that are striking, distinctive for both eyes and ears. This method might be called synchronizing image and sound.

5.   Through practice, the aim is to see and hear the musical structure of a work, to detect, while reading, details that may

be barely audible. In this way, reading a score enhances the musical experience. Concentrating on a single line, and counting to keep your place, are mere steps on the road to this end, which will be a truly musical reading of a score.

These five methods are listed in the order in which they should be practiced, and each one is examined in some detail below. Chapter 6 then provides excerpts from scores as the first examples for practice. They are arranged in order of increasing difficulty. The excerpts were chosen because they are well known and many readers are likely to own recordings of them. They are all available on inexpensive recordings and several publishers issue the music in study or pocket scores.

Following a single part

Many first-time score readers are perplexed by the many lines, the large number of parts: What do I hear? What should I read? It is therefore wise to begin with compositions in which one part is prominent. A voice part is most suitable, not only for the ease of tracking the text, but also because the timbre of the human voice is distinct. In scores of baroque music the voice parts, both solo and choral, always appear above the continuo, that is, above the cello and bass part or parts. In later music voice parts may be printed above the first violin part. A single instrumental part will also stand out clearly.

The first example (see figure 25 and p. 92) combines a vocal and instrumental solo part. The solo violin begins, rising above the sustained notes of the string orchestra's violins and violas. A steady, pulsating pizzicato accompaniment by the basses emphasizes the great calm of this music. After a few measures, the alto soloist (A) enters; her melody is interwoven with that of the solo violin. Readers can follow either line, or may be able to trace both melodies simultaneously. In this piece the bass line also stands out clearly, but it makes more sense to concentrate on the two solos because they are musically more important. In other works, especially in baroque music, it would be appropriate to follow the bass line—as a basso continuo it is the foundation that is prominent and easily heard.

Figure 26 is an excerpt from Corelli's "Christmas Concerto," featuring violin parts that weave in and out. Here the bass line stands out

25. Voice part with text and instrumental solo part (J. S. Bach, "Erbarme dich, mein Gott," Aria No. 47 from *The Passion According to St. Matthew*)

26. Following the bass line (Corelli, Concerto Grosso Op. 6, No. 8, "Christmas Concerto")

more clearly. Solo and tutti violins play the same music. Harpsichords accompany both solo and tutti groups.

To practice following an instrumental solo part, turn to Beethoven's *Romanze* in F Major for violin and orchestra (see figure 27). As customary, the solo violin part is printed above the orchestra's first violin part.

27. Following an instrumental solo part (Beethoven, *Romanze* in F Major)

One feature of concertos for a solo instrument and orchestra is the cadenza. It offers soloists opportunities to show their artistry without orchestral accompaniment. Originally a cadenza was meant to be improvised, but in time it became primarily a vehicle for virtuosic display. Though it may give the impression of an improvisation, the performer more likely worked it out and practiced it thoroughly at home. By Beethoven's time, composers often wrote their own cadenzas. Famous virtuosos also composed cadenzas which sometimes were published for the use of other soloists.

Early cadenzas often were little more than elaborate flourishes just before the end of a movement. Later, cadenzas continued to be interpolated at that point. Before Beethoven they rarely were included in the written or printed score. Their place merely was indicated by a fermata over a rest in the orchestra parts. The cadenza might end on a long trill, notated in the solo part with another fermata (see figure 28).

As the nineteenth century progressed, cadenzas (written by the composer) often became an integral part of the movement and therefore were printed in their entirety. Beethoven's Fifth Piano Concerto furnishes an example (see figure 29). But at this time it apparently was not yet taken for granted that the composer had provided a cadenza,

28. Cadenza in a solo concerto (Haydn, Cello Concerto in D Major)

for a footnote in the score announces "Non si fa una Cadenza" (do not make a cadenza), because the composer has supplied it.

Even in works without vocal or instrumental solos, one part is likely to stand out. Often the first violin has the principal motivic material. Because it is the highest string part it may also be the most prominent. If the composition includes a chorus, the highest voice, the "soprano," most often attracts attention.

Chamber music scores

After following scores with solo voices or instruments, next examine scores with only a few parts, none of which clearly dominates. Chamber music scores serve this purpose, also many orchestral scores of the baroque and early classic periods, as well as some later compositions. When reading such a score, try not to insist on focusing on one part but follow whatever line is most clearly heard at any given moment. Three examples are provided for practice: a piano piece, a work for string orchestra, and a chamber music piece with piano.

Chopin's "Minute Waltz" is, of course, not a score in the usual sense, being a piano solo (see figure 30 and p. 119). Nevertheless, reading both the main line in the right hand and the left-hand accompani-

29. Cadenza written out by the composer (Beethoven, Fifth Piano Concerto)

ment requires a similar reading technique. The fast tempo adds to the difficulty.

The second example is taken from Mozart's *Eine kleine Nachtmusik*. It is scored for first and second violins, viola, cello, and double bass (see figure 31 and p. 124). Whether it was intended for solo strings or string orchestra is unknown; today it is performed either way. The

30. Piano composition (Chopin, Waltz in D-flat Major, "Minute Waltz")

31. Chamber music score (Mozart, *Eine kleine Nachtmusik*, second movement)

first violin leads throughout, so the reader might concentrate on that part. At times the other instruments also have some melodic interest.

Schubert's "Trout" Quintet calls for an unusual combination of instruments: violin, viola, cello, bass, and piano (see figure 32). Try to follow whatever instrument leads at a given time. At the beginning, these are piano and violin, later also the other instruments. Still, the piano part helps most of the time to keep track of the music. The excerpt for practicing, beginning on page 133, is not from the first but the fourth movement, which gave the quintet its popular name. It consists of six variations on a theme from Schubert's song "Die Forelle" (The trout). The first violin presents the theme, which then moves on to the other instruments: piano, then viola, next cello and double bass. In Variation 4 it bounces back and forth between piano and the high strings. At this point the theme appears in the minor mode and is treated rather freely, so that it is not quite so easily recognized. Variation 5 belongs to the cello; in Variation 6, again merry and fast, violin and cello play the theme.

32. Chamber music with piano (Schubert, "The Trout" Quintet)

Counting beats and measures

Before turning to more complex scores, consider a very different approach to following a score: counting the beats and measures, or keeping time. At first this mechanical approach may seem of little musical value, for it fails to deal with the music's sound and formal organization. In an extreme case, you could count measures with your eyes closed and still know where to find a certain place in the score. Moreover, by concentrating on counting, the eyes, freed from following melodic lines or motives, may detect some formal features that are difficult to hear. In short, the counting method has its advantages.

This system, though it does not involve precise note reading, can be appropriate in several situations:

- You have not yet had much practice in note reading;
- You can read notes fairly well, but the score is very complex;
- You absolutely must not lose your place, your orientation in the score; and
- You want insight into the musical structure, rather than practice following individual lines.

Whether the counting method is appropriate also depends on the kind of music under consideration. It is most useful when the tempo is very fast and when the texture is undifferentiated, meaning no lines are prominent. Of course, the meter, with emphasis on the strong beats, must be easily heard. Figure 33 lists the most important metric patterns in music since 1600. Some music of our time, even if it is not avant garde, has such complex and changing rhythm patterns that they can be hard to detect.

An example that clearly calls for the counting method is figure 34, from a Beethoven string quartet. The tempo is presto, and though the passage is marked *pianissimo*, the accent on every downbeat can be heard clearly, though the texture is uniform and undifferentiated.

Figure 35, on the other hand, would be quite unsuitable for this method: the tempo is slow (Adagio), the metric pulse is obscured by the many suspensions (notes held across bar lines), and the first violin plays a melodic line that is easy to follow.

Music that is void of regular accentuation would not be a candidate for the counting method. This applies to much pre-1600 music, though dance music of all ages necessarily has regular, recurring accents. The rhythm of much early vocal music, especially sacred music and social music such as madrigals, is governed by the accentuation of the text. In renaissance vocal music this may result in sudden changes

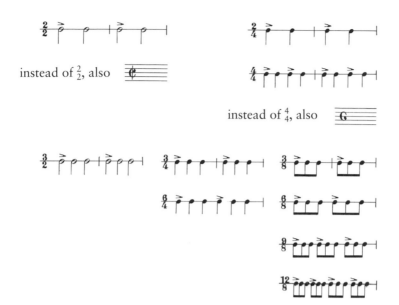

33. Rhythm patterns and time signatures

34. Beethoven, String Quartet in C-sharp Minor, Op. 131

35. Beethoven, String Quartet in C-sharp Minor, Op. 131

from duple to triple rhythm. Figure 36a is taken from a transcription into modern notation of a *Stabat mater* by Palestrina (d. 1594). For a long time he was considered the foremost composer of church music. The work is scored for double chorus. In this edition the original clefs have been placed in front of the modern clefs. A modern time signature, 2/2 3/2, implies that the meter frequently changes from one to the other, depending on the text. But applied to Palestrina's music the transcription with modern time signatures and the accents they imply give a totally misleading picture, as shown in the second measure: the accents based on the text are different from the normal accents in a measure of 3/2 time. Three-two meter would result in syncopation that goes counter to the text accents. Other editions of such music avoid bar lines *in* each part but place them *between* parts. That way they are an aid to counting but do not suggest an accent on each "downbeat," so common in later music.

Much twentieth-century music presents difficulties for readers trying to use the counting method due to frequent changes of time signature. When these are coupled with complex rhythms, the counting method no longer works, though careful observing of the ever-changing time signatures is a must (see figure 37).

Synchronizing image and sound

It is not always practical to count continuously. A complicated score may challenge the untrained listener, and there may be outside disturbances or interferences. During a recording session, for instance, a brief conversation between recording supervisor and engineer, or the sudden discovery of a small problem, may interrupt the counting. In such cases it is important to find your place again quickly, to reestablish the connection between sound and printed music, between hearing and seeing. To accomplish this it is best to just listen for a short time while trying to relate the basic sound quality to its reflection in the score. You might hear that the strings have many fast notes, that the brass is silent, and

36. Modern transcription of renaissance vocal music (a) with bar lines (Palestrina, *Stabat mater*) and (b) with lines drawn between parts (Monteverdi, "Lasciate mi morire")

that the woodwinds are playing sustained notes. If such a moment occurs repeatedly, you may want to wait for a clearer, more drastic cue, such as an entrance of all the woodwinds, or a place where the first violins play by themselves, or a solo passage on a wind instrument, or a striking entrance by a percussion instrument such as the cymbals. Figure 38, showing an entrance of woodwinds and brass, is such a place, where image and sound can be synchronized easily.

Of course, the reverse approach is also possible. You can look in the score for such a distinctive place, being reasonably sure that it has not been reached yet, and wait until you hear it. For this purpose it is best to find several such places in the score and listen for any corre-

37. Score from the early twentieth century shows frequent changes of time signature related to complex rhythms (Stravinsky, "Sacrificial Dance" from *The Rite of Spring*)

sponding places in the music. Practicing this synchronization method regularly will help a great deal.

While listening and following a score, you may encounter a passage that stands out to the eye but is hardly noticed by the ear. For example, the sound of rapid passage work may be covered up by the

38. Synchronizing image and sound (Wagner, Prelude to *Die Meistersinger von Nürnberg*)

massive sound of the rest of the orchestra. In the last measure of figure 38 the strings play such a passage, an ascending scale. It looks prominent on the score page but is a fairly insignificant detail in the overall sound. The same example includes a harp part that may catch the eye but in performance often is barely audible. Timpani also may play very softly; they are not always heard as clearly as we tend to expect. The same is sometimes true of horn entrances.

Fast accompaniment figures in less important parts may also look more important than they are. Figure 39 is an excerpt from Schumann's Piano Concerto. The most important musical line is given to the first violin and to the left-hand piano part.

39. Visually prominent accompaniment figuration detracts from seeing the main part (Schumann, Piano Concerto, first movement)

Conversely, we will find entrances that are inconspicuous on the score page but that clearly stand out in sound. Figure 40 is taken from the last movement of Beethoven's Fifth Symphony. Here the brass instruments have an important entrance. After a *pianissimo* passage by the rest of the orchestra there is a short crescendo, after which trumpets and trombones (along with the full orchestra) come in *fortissimo*. It is a startling entrance that is less obvious in the printed score. Here the careful dynamic markings should not be overlooked. The direction "*pp cresc. - - - ff*" signals an unusually powerful increase in volume by the full orchestra.

40. Beethoven, Fifth Symphony, fourth movement

Musical reading of a score

So far we have investigated four ways of approaching score reading: to follow a single part, to trace several parts as they appear to be prominent, to count whole measures if they are clearly accented, and to concentrate on places that stand out visually or aurally.

As a longer composition unfolds, we are likely to use more than one of these ways. For example, we might follow a solo passage by the first oboe, note for note, then read the answer to this passage coming from another instrument. Later, there may be rapid modulations (changes from one key to another), or short motives may move quickly from one group of instruments to another. With so much going on, at a fast tempo, we may revert to counting, just to keep up. Even seasoned score readers will find it challenging to keep their place in the Scherzo of Beethoven's Ninth Symphony, due to its breakneck speed and the rather uniform appearance of the score page. Especially at a first hearing it will be best simply to count whole measures. But if we lose track we may look for places that are easily recognized by our eyes and ears—the synchronizing approach. Having succeeded with this, we may return to another way of following a score.

For further practice, ten excerpts are provided in chapter 6, arranged in order of increasing difficulty. By way of introducing these examples we shall again take up various ways of following a score, from first getting our bearings in it to our comprehension of the music's structure. We can hardly arrive at such comprehension at a first hearing; some closer study of the work, score in hand, will be needed.

In the Mozart example (pp. 150–161) we can either keep track of individual parts or rely on the counting method, preferably both at the same time. Most important material is given to the strings, but as the movement unfolds the winds also have important things to say. Strings and winds are mostly contrasted rather than integrated. In his Fifth Symphony Beethoven shows more finesse in exploring the timbres of individual instruments and groups of instruments (pp. 162–175). It is rewarding to trace the famous "knocking-at-the-door" motive ♪ ♪♪♪ | 𝅝 through many parts.

Brahms's Fourth Symphony (pp. 176–199) is scored for virtually the same orchestra as Beethoven's Fifth. Its stylistic origins also lie in Beethoven. (An even closer relationship exists between Brahms's First and Beethoven's Fifth.) Brahms's treatment of the winds generally resembles Beethoven's, though Brahms uses more polyphonic interplay.

Perhaps the chief objective of studying scores is to obtain an in-depth understanding of the music, a better comprehension of what we are hearing, including musical form. It would be difficult to gain such understanding solely by listening.

The vertical and horizontal aspects of form or structure need explanation. The vertical deals with harmonic progression, an important ingredient affecting the design of a composition. To recognize harmonic structure in a score is not easy because harmony is produced by the simultaneous sound of many instruments, often including transposing instruments. Reading these vertical structures presents challenges to readers who have not studied music theory that includes harmony. Harmonic analysis therefore goes beyond the goals of this book. Horizontal structures, on the other hand, are easier to recognize and to follow. They apply to melody, phrases and motives, and rhythm, though here, too, readers need some acquaintance with music theory. Nevertheless, in this chapter's last example we shall try to hear and see how motives travel from instrument to instrument, and how they are developed and otherwise modified (figure 41). Some readers will find this difficult, but they will certainly obtain an impression of the artistry, the great sense for tone color, with which Wagner composed his Prelude to *Tristan*. Our examination is restricted to the first five pages of the score and looks into only one aspect of the work's structure.

According to Wagner's own commentary, this Prelude represents the unquenchable longing that Tristan and Isolde feel for each other. It is expressed through a gradual, powerful increase in the music's tension, followed by a rapid sinking back into the calm of the opening. A distinctive, new feature in *Tristan* is the music's steady flow. Instead of breaks in the melodic lines, instead of partial endings and sudden new entrances, we hear gradual, smooth transitions and a continuous forward motion. Every chord seems to demand a resolution, only to lead to another chord with the same tension. Among the many aspects of the Prelude that invite analysis, consider the use of three melodic fragments or motives:

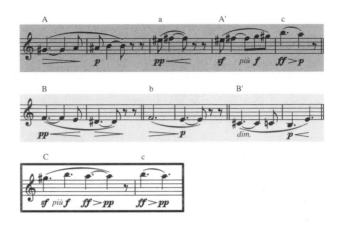

The Prelude begins with two motives that often recur throughout the opera (or music drama, a term Wagner preferred). One motive consists of an ascending (A), the other of a descending chromatic scale segment (B). The two related motives represent longing love (A) and sorrow (B). In the second measure the two motives are combined; in a way they summarize the drama's essence. Both also occur in a shortened form: a rising (a) and falling (b) half step. Later there is a further variant of A, marked here A'. It consists of A and a further motive, c, a shortened variant of C. While A sounds like a question, C has the character of an answer. Beginning in measure 17 (see figure 41), a sweeping melody comes from the cellos. It differs from A and B in its scalewise motion and introduces a more positive, hopeful element. We have not given it a special symbol. In the short excerpt quoted here, motive A and its variants appear about forty times, motive B twenty-five times, and C thirteen times. Hardly a single measure is without at least one of these motives. Most often A and B or their variants are heard simultaneously. They are the threads with which the music fabric is woven—loose at first, then increasingly dense.

41. Musical reading of a score (Wagner, Prelude to *Tristan and Isolde*, beginning) (*continues on pages 86–89*)

6 Examples for Practicing Score Reading

The selections offered here for practice in reading and hearing are arranged in order of increasing difficulty. All the methods described before can be applied to them.

Obviously, these few short examples serve only as starters. They were chosen because they are well known and easily available on recordings. After having studied these compositions, practice further with scores and recordings of comparable degrees of difficulty (see p. 243 for suggestions).

Johann Sebastian Bach: "Erbarme dich, mein Gott" (Have mercy, O Lord), Aria No. 47 from *The Passion According to St. Matthew*, BWV 244, Part II

Ludwig van Beethoven: *Romanze* in F Major, Op. 50, No. 2, for violin and orchestra

Frédéric Chopin: Waltz in D-flat Major, Op. 64, No. 1, for piano, the "Minute Waltz"

Wolfgang Amadeus Mozart: *Eine kleine Nachtmusik*, Serenade in G Major, K. 525, fourth movement

Franz Schubert: Quintet in A Major for piano, violin, viola, cello, and double bass, "The Trout," fourth movement

Wolfgang Amadeus Mozart: Symphony in C Major, K. 551, "Jupiter," excerpt from the first movement

Ludwig van Beethoven: Symphony No. 5 in C minor, Op. 67, excerpt from the first movement

Johannes Brahms: Symphony No. 4 in E minor, Op. 98, excerpt from the first movement

Richard Wagner: Prelude to *Tristan and Isolde*

Igor Stravinsky: *The Firebird*, ballet suite, 1945, excerpt

To facilitate following these scores, those vocal or instrumental parts that stand out—those that are easily heard—are shaded on the printed page.

Johann Sebastian Bach: "Erbarme dich, mein Gott" (Have mercy, O Lord), Aria No. 47 from The Passion According to St. Matthew, BWV 244, Part II

THE WORK   Bach performed the *St. Matthew Passion* for the first time on Good Friday, 1729, in Leipzig. The text is taken from the Gospel according to Matthew, augmented by chorale texts and by baroque poetry by Picander (the pen name of Christian Friedrich Henrici).

The work is scored for two separate bodies of sound, each group having its orchestra, chorus, and organ part. There is one narrator, the Evangelist; other singers represent individuals involved in the action, such as Petrus (Peter). Additional soloists sing arias with texts by Picander. These interrupt the drama of the Gospel account; they are contemplative, expressing emotions caused by the story. These arias provide points of rest and can be compared to the painted or carved images seen on the stations of the cross frequently found in Catholic churches and elsewhere in Catholic countries.

The alto aria "Erbarme dich" is such an interruption. After Peter's threefold denial ("I do not know the man"), the Evangelist continues: "Then Peter remembered the saying of Jesus 'Before the cock crows, you will deny me three times.' And he went out and wept bitterly." The aria follows at this point. It is a moving interpretation of Picander's text, musically expressed by solo violin and alto voice. Strings accompany, *piano sempre* (always *piano*), while the basses' pizzicato line supplies a steady heart beat.

An instrumental postlude is identical to the prelude or introduction and is not written out again. At the aria's end, the words *Dal segno al* ⌒ indicate that the prelude is to be repeated, from the sign 𝄋 above the first bar line to the fermata ⌒ in measure eight.

SCORING   In addition to solo voice and solo violin, the aria calls for the accompaniment of a string orchestra, the bass line of which (cello and double bass) is plucked (pizzicato) throughout. The bottom line of the score, *Organo e Continuo*, is played by the bass instruments of the string orchestra and the chord instrument, here the organ. Figures below that line show the organist what chords to play.

The direction "Coro I" tells that here the first orchestra and first organ are to play—the complete score of the *Passion* includes two orchestras, two continuo organs, and two choruses.

See page 67 for suggestions about reading this score.

Ludwig van Beethoven: Romanze *in F Major, Op. 50, No. 2, for violin and orchestra*

THE WORK   Beethoven composed this *Romanze* and the one in G major in 1803, two years before his Violin Concerto. It is an attractive, melodious work—*cantabile* means songlike—which accounts for its great popularity. The violin part consists of one melody line throughout, whereas the *Romanze* in G Major explores the violin's capacity for polyphonic playing (double stops). As indicated by the alla breve time signature, or cut time, the basic counting unit is the half note rather than quarter note, thereby avoiding too slow a tempo. A calm, flowing quality should prevail.

SCORING   The soloist is in the foreground; the orchestra essentially functions as accompaniment, which accounts for its modest, conservative size. Cellos and double basses play in unison, though in Beethoven's time it was customary for bass players to simplify their parts. Thus in measures 96–99 (eight to five measures from the end) they might have played eighth notes or quarter notes instead of the repeated sixteenth notes printed. The winds have little music of importance. Second flute and clarinets are absent, and two horns in F are the only transposing instruments; they sound a fifth lower than written. The first violin part keeps to a fairly low register; the flute frequently doubles it an octave higher. A generally mellow orchestral sound characterizes this piece.

See page 68 for suggestions about reading this score.

Frédéric Chopin: Waltz in D-flat Major, Op. 64, No. 1, for piano, the "Minute Waltz"

THE WORK   Waltzes were heard in Austria and southern Germany in the late eighteenth century. Two dance types that preceded the waltz were the *Deutsche* and *Ländler*. The waltz became enormously popular after the Congress of Vienna (1814–1815), later especially through the works of the father and son Johann Strauss. Its popularity went hand-in-hand with nineteenth-century social revolutions. At first it was a dance of the common people, especially in Vienna where a veritable waltz mania broke out. Upper society initially was shocked by the waltz, a fast couple dance in which the partners whirled around in close embrace. At the Prussian court in Berlin, waltzing never was allowed at official court balls, and in France it never achieved the popularity it enjoyed in Vienna.

In time, a distinction developed between waltzes for dancing and waltzes for listening, or concert waltzes. Chopin's waltzes straddle the line, though most belong to the concert type. Schumann once remarked about a Chopin waltz that it was not appropriate for dancing unless at least half the ladies on the dance floor were countesses.

Actually, the form of the "Minute Waltz" resembles that of many Viennese waltzes meant for dancing. There is a short introduction, followed by the first part consisting of two eight-measure periods, each of which is repeated. A middle section follows, similarly structured but contrasting in character. Part one is then repeated.

An interesting feature is the juxtaposition of the typical and distinct triple rhythm in the left hand with duple rhythm figures in the right hand. This occurs in the introduction, in the first four measures of the first part, and again in the second part.

See page 70 for suggestions about reading this score.

Wolfgang Amadeus Mozart: Eine kleine Nachtmusik, *Serenade in G Major, K. 525, fourth movement*

THE WORK   Mozart wrote this serenade, one of the most popular compositions of the classic period, on 10 August 1787. In his hand-written catalog of his works he refers to it as having five movements, but only four have come down to us. We know nothing about the fifth movement, a minuet to follow the first movement, or about the occasion for which Mozart wrote the work; we do know that his serenades generally were written on commission. The title is Mozart's own, found in his catalog.

Serenades from the age of Viennese Classicism mostly were light, social music, often intended for outdoor performance. The more formal plan of this serenade clearly relates it to that of the symphony.

SCORING   Performance by five solo instruments is possible: first and second violins, viola, cello, and bass. In chamber music this combination of instruments is rare, but it is normal for a string orchestra, with several players on each part.

See page 71 for suggestions about reading this score.

129 Coda

Franz Schubert: Quintet in A Major for piano, violin, viola, cello, and double bass, "The Trout," fourth movement

THE WORK   This charming, vibrant composition dates from 1819. Today it is one of Schubert's most loved creations and one of the most popular of all works of chamber music. He wrote it at the suggestion of Sylvester Paumgartner in Steyr, where Schubert and his friend, the baritone Johann Michael Vogl, had spent the summer. Apparently Paumgartner requested that the composition include a set of variations on Schubert's lied "Die Forelle" (The trout) of 1817, a song of which Paumgartner was extremely fond.

Schubert inserted the variations movement between the Scherzo and Finale of what would otherwise have been a normal four-movement quintet. His use of the song theme extends beyond the variations movement; its poetic idea permeates the entire composition. The story is simple: A passer-by watches a fisherman who, in a clear brook, tries to catch a trout. He succeeds, but only after muddying the water with his fishing rod. The music of Schubert's quintet, however, implies a happy ending: the fish regains its freedom.

SCORING   The particular combination of instruments may reflect the players who were available in Paumgartner's home: piano, violin, viola, cello, and bass. They are arranged on the score page in the customary order according to their range, with the piano part at the bottom. The string bass sounds an octave lower than written.

See page 72 for suggestions about reading this score.

Wolfgang Amadeus Mozart: Symphony in C Major, K. 551, "Jupiter," excerpt from the first movement

THE WORK   Mozart completed this symphony (the title is not his own but was given to it after his death) on 10 August 1788, exactly one year after *Eine kleine Nachtmusik*. He must have committed the score to paper in a very short time, because the symphony preceding the "Jupiter," the G Minor Symphony, is dated 25 July. He completed the E-flat Major Symphony, the first of the three late symphonies, on 26 June. Thus three symphonies that in every respect are among the most significant compositions of the classic period were written in as little as three months.

SCORING   Mozart's symphonies have no standard scoring; it even varies among these last three. What they have in common, in addition to the strings, are one flute, two bassoons, and two horns. In addition to these, the E-flat Major Symphony calls for two clarinets; the G Minor and "Jupiter" Symphonies require two oboes. Trumpets and timpani join in the E-flat Major and "Jupiter" Symphonies.

In Mozart's autograph score the order of instruments follows the Italian practice of the time: high, non-transposing instruments appear above the low and the transposing ones. This results in the following arrangement on the score page, in descending order: first and second violins, viola, flute, first and second oboes, first and second bassoons, first and second horns, first and second trumpets, and timpani. Modern editions bring the arrangement with which we are familiar today. The trumpets (Mozart still calls them clarini) do not transpose: they are C trumpets, and the symphony's key is C major. The horns also are written in C; actually they are "low C" horns, sounding an octave lower than written.

See page 82 for suggestions about reading this score.

Ludwig van Beethoven: Symphony No. 5 in C minor, Op. 67, excerpt from the first movement

THE WORK   Whereas Mozart wrote many of his symphonies in an incredibly short time, Beethoven tended to work quite differently; the composition of a symphony occupied him over long periods. His sketch books, many of which have been preserved, help in tracing this process. They show that his first sketches for the Fifth go back to 1803, but he did most of the work in late 1807 and early 1808. His Sixth Symphony was completed at about the same time, so that most likely Beethoven worked on both scores simultaneously or alternately.

The Fifth sometimes has been called the "Fate" Symphony, a title based on the composer's alleged remark about the opening measures: "Thus fate knocks at the door." That remark was quoted by Beethoven's pupil Anton Schindler whose recollections are generally unreliable.

Beethoven's Fifth is among his most popular works. A 1913 set of disks was the first complete recording of any symphony, and it has been recorded countless times since then. The first performance took place at an all-Beethoven concert on 22 December 1808 in Vienna's Theater an der Wien. This was a public concert, or "academy," the length of which would seem monstrous to us. In addition to the Fifth, the program featured the Sixth Symphony, the Fourth Piano Concerto, the *Choral Phantasy*, and parts of the Mass in C Major. Beethoven, who was the pianist, also improvised on that instrument. All works were receiving their first performances, quite different from the usual concert programs of our time.

SCORING   The orchestration for the first three movements includes strings, the doubled woodwinds customary to the time, two horns, two trumpets, and timpani. For the last movement Beethoven added a piccolo flute, contrabassoon, and three trombones. The additions point in the direction of later nineteenth-century orchestral writing.

The first printed score appeared in 1826; individual parts had been published in 1809. In the score, timpani are at the top of the page, followed by trumpets ("clarini") and horns. Below these, woodwinds and strings occupy the places customary today. The E-flat horns transpose down a major sixth, B-flat clarinets down a whole tone. The piccolo sounds an octave higher, the contrabassoon an octave lower than written.

See page 82 for suggestions about reading this score.

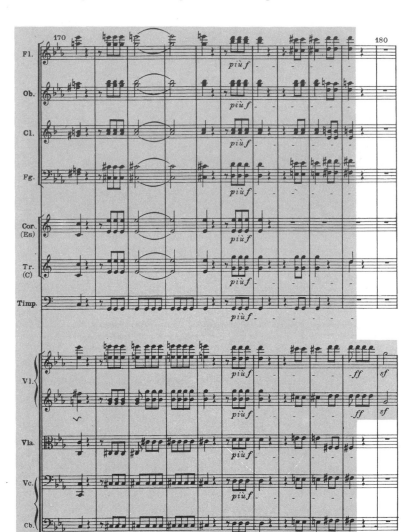

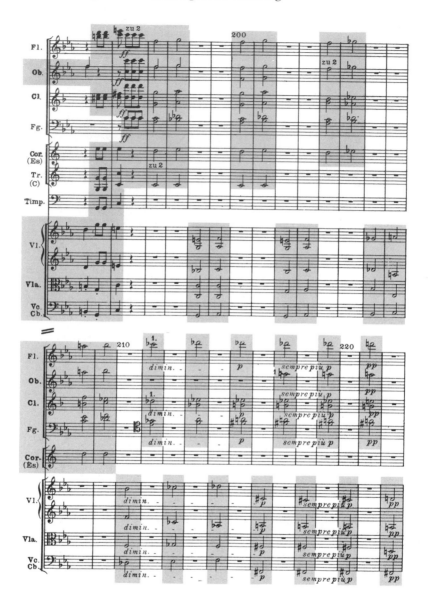

Johannes Brahms: Symphony No. 4 in E minor, Op. 98, excerpt from the first movement

THE WORK   Brahms's Fourth Symphony, his last, was written during the summers of 1884 and 1885. Beethoven, in his last symphony, went far beyond his earlier ones in regard to form and content. Brahms's Fourth, on the other hand, in some ways harks back to earlier epochs, incorporating some early traditions of form and instrumental sound. An elegiac, romantic mood characterizes the first movement, which accounts for the name "Elegiac" Symphony, sometimes given to the work. Melodies of the second movement vaguely suggest the sound of medieval music, of the so-called church modes. The fourth movement reveals a unique structural concept: thirty variations of eight measures each present a simple theme in the manner of a chaconne, with every variation displaying a new sound picture.

SCORING   Brahms's symphonies largely use the instrumentation of the classic period with paired woodwinds as a basis. To this base he adds four horns, two trumpets, three trombones, and timpani. A contrabassoon joins in all but the Second Symphony; the Fourth adds piccolo and triangle. At the end of the nineteenth century this lineup of instruments was conservative, and that is the label that has been applied to much of Brahms's music. After more than a hundred years, however, that label has lost some of its significance, and it certainly does not imply a value judgment.

In this excerpt, among the woodwinds, the piccolo transposes up an octave, the contrabassoon down an octave. The A clarinets sound a minor third lower than written. Brahms continued to use valveless horns. In the first movement are two horns in E (transposing a minor sixth down) and two in C (an octave down). By combining two pairs of horns in different keys it is possible to counteract to some extent the limitations of the natural horns.

See page 82 for suggestions about reading this score.

Allegro non troppo

Richard Wagner: Prelude to Tristan and Isolde

THE WORK   Wagner's music drama is among the rare works in music history that both mark the end of a style epoch and usher in a new age. Wagner introduced drastic changes into the medium of opera; his music dramas no longer follow the arrangement of traditional "number operas" that consisted of a succession of recitatives, arias, choruses, and other self-contained pieces. Instead the composer provided a steady, uninterrupted musical flow in which the orchestra, instead of merely accompanying the singers, easily equals them in importance. The orchestra participates in the dramatic action and often expresses intense, sometimes violent emotions. This new approach reaches its high point in *Tristan*. In his *Recollections of Ludwig Schnorr von Carolsfeld*, Wagner explained the significance of his method, referring specifically to the role of what came to be called *leitmotive*, or leading motives: short musical motives that "continually appear, change, are combined, separated, again are blended, finally struggle with each other and almost devour each other. Because of their emotional significance they require most careful harmonization and orchestration."

Our analysis in chapter 5 of the Prelude's opening is based on Wagner's description. The music expresses "most profound emotion," inspired by the drama's inner action: "Tristan presents his bride-to-be to his king, Marke, who also is his uncle. . . . The emotions of the pair run from subdued feelings of unquenchable desire, from tender, trembling sentiment, to the most powerful confession of hopeless love. Their emotions reflect all phases of a heated struggle in which there can be no victory, until at last they subside, sinking down, as in death." This description is reflected in the music's tremendous, steadily growing intensity up to measure 83, after which, in twenty-eight measures, it diminishes, returning to complete silence.

SCORING   Wagner employs balanced woodwind, brass, and string sections; all three contribute equally to his subtle handling of the orchestra. He calls for triple woodwinds: to the two oboes he adds the English horn (sounding a fifth lower than written), and to the clarinets he adds the bass clarinet. The last is notated in the G clef; it sounds an octave and minor third lower than written. Like Brahms, Wagner writes for valveless horns in two keys, thereby increasing the notes available to them. Trumpets in F sound a fourth higher than written.

By adding a bass tuba to the three trombones, the composer achieves a full sound in the low brass group. The harp, whose part is indicated on the first page of the score, does not play in the Prelude.

See page 83 for suggestions for reading this score.

allmählich im Zeitmaß etwas zurückhaltend
poco a poco ritenuto

Igor Stravinsky: The Firebird, *ballet suite, 1945, excerpt*

THE WORK   Today Stravinsky is considered a leader of twentieth-century music. He greatly affected its development during the first few decades. He called his ballet a "choreographic fairy tale," based on incidents in a Russian folktale. From the ballet music, completed in 1910, Stravinsky prepared an orchestra version for concert performance in 1911. Further revisions date from 1919 and 1945. The following excerpt is taken from the 1945 version.

The Firebird suite has remained one of Stravinsky's most popular compositions. Stylistically it belongs to the period around the turn of the century, an age of transition reflecting the confluence of many musical trends. Evident in *The Firebird* is the influence of the Russian composers Rimsky-Korsakov and Mussorgsky, but also that of French Impressionism. In addition it carries the characteristic element of infectious Slavic rhythms.

The Introduction depicts a blossoming magic garden. Next comes the "Dance of the Firebird," which reaches its climax with the adoration of the bird.

SCORING   Strings and winds are represented by traditional forces: doubled woodwinds, four horns, two trumpets, three trombones, and bass tuba. More innovative is the makeup of the percussion section, though this becomes evident only after this excerpt: small (snare) and large (bass) drums, cymbal, triangle, tambourine, and xylophone. Piano and harp complete the instrumentation. Two A clarinets and four F horns are the transposing instruments. The key signatures on the first page show that not all instruments play in the same key. One group—strings, trombones, bassoons, and clarinets—has the key signature for A-flat minor; clarinets have the enharmonic equivalent of G-sharp minor. Flutes, oboes, piano, and harp have no key signature, indicating C major or A minor. As usual, trumpet and horn parts are written without key signature.

Introduction

1b. Prelude and Dance of the Firebird

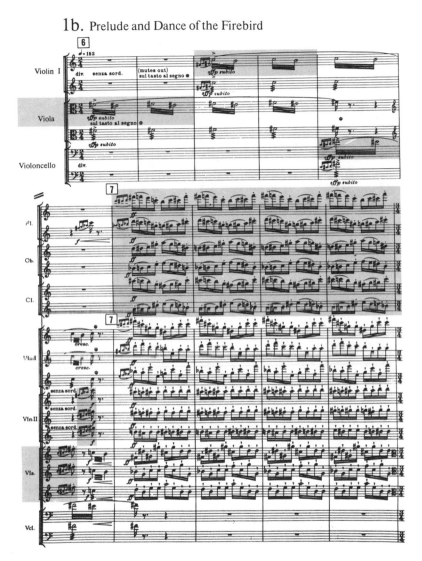

1c. Variations (Firebird)

A few scores recommended for further practice

1. SCORES WITH A SINGLE PROMINENT PART
   Voice part:
   > Arias from J. S. Bach's cantatas and Passions, also from his *Christmas Oratorio*
   >
   > Arias from Haydn's oratorios *The Seasons* and *The Creation*
   >
   > Orchestra songs by Richard Strauss (*Four Last Songs*) and Gustav Mahler (*Songs of a Wayfarer, Songs on the Death of Children, Seven Late Songs*)

   Instrumental part:
   > Violin concertos by J. S. Bach, Mozart, Beethoven, Mendelssohn, and Brahms
   >
   > Piano concertos by Mozart, Beethoven, Schumann, Grieg, and Brahms

2. SCORES WITH FEW PARTS
   Chamber music:
   > String quartets by Haydn, Mozart, Beethoven, Schubert, Dvořák, and Bartók
   >
   > Wind serenades by Mozart

   Small orchestral works:
   > Concerti grossi by Handel and Corelli
   >
   > Orchestra suites by J. S. Bach
   >
   > Early symphonies of Haydn and Mozart

3. MEDIUM-SIZED ORCHESTRAL WORKS
   > Mozart middle and late symphonies (K. 385, 425, 504, 543, 550, 551)
   >
   > Haydn symphonies Nos. 93–104
   >
   > Symphonies by Beethoven, Schumann, and Brahms

4. LARGE ORCHESTRAL WORKS
   > Symphonic poems by Richard Strauss
   >
   > Symphonies by Bruckner and Mahler
   >
   > Mussorgsky *Pictures at an Exhibition* in Ravel's instrumentation
   >
   > Orchestral works by Debussy
   >
   > Ballet scores by Stravinsky

7 Orchestras and Conductors

In a typical orchestra each string part is played by several musicians and wind parts are soloistic. The term *chamber music*, in modern usage, refers to music played with one person on each part. Less specific is the term *chamber orchestra*, simply meaning a small orchestra.

In ancient Greece, "orchestra" was the name given to the semicircular space for dancers and singers in front of the theater's "scene," or outdoor stage. When opera emerged as a new art form around 1600, it was intended to be a re-creation of the drama of antiquity. The musicians' performance space included a roughly semicircular area in front of the stage, still called orchestra today (see figure 42). Not until the mid-eighteenth century was the name of the area also given to the performing ensemble. Before then, it would have been inappropriate to think of the group of players as an entity, a unified body; rather, the single player was the focus of attention. Before 1600, during the Renaissance, instrumental music rarely had more than one player to a part; if it did, that part would be played on different instruments. One style characteristic of instrumental music before 1750 was the improvised embellishing or ornamenting of a part, something that several players cannot do simultaneously. Tied to the emergence of the orchestra, then, is the abolishing of improvisation. (An exception was the realization of the continuo part by the harpsichord player.) In a way, this amounts to a loss of creative participation in performance.

As time went on, musicians played from written or printed parts that became increasingly specific, containing more and more instructions as to exactly how the music should be played. In our own time we can observe a trend in the opposite direction: many modern compositions again offer opportunities for improvisation.

42. Stage and orchestra in a baroque opera house
(Naples court theater, 1747)

Another feature that set earlier music apart from orchestral music was the freedom of choice of instruments. Which instruments participated often depended on the local availability of players and instruments. Before the eighteenth century this adaptability was the norm; in later orchestral music it would be unusual, for instance, to give the flute part of a symphony to another instrument. All these features contributed to a greater fixation of compositional details, giving the player less freedom and therefore requiring discipline and subordination to the instructions of composer and conductor.

Until the mid-seventeenth century, wind instruments dominated larger ensembles; after that, strings rapidly moved into the first place, generally with several players on a part. At the court of Louis XIV, the most prestigious ensemble still was the one named The King's Twenty-Four Violinists, calling attention to individual players rather than to the group as a whole. In other French ensembles of the time the strings were augmented by two oboes and one bassoon; they became the nucleus of the orchestra's wind section. They doubled the highest and lowest parts but also played independent lines, as in the minuet, allegedly danced by the king for the first time in 1653. Even in nineteenth-century symphonies, the minuet or scherzo often included a trio section given to the woodwinds. Italian string orchestras normally had first and second violin, viola, cello, and bass parts. The basses mostly played cello parts an octave lower. Well into the eighteenth century, French string orchestras included a second viola part.

Numbers and types of instruments

The kinds of instruments that constituted orchestras at various times governed the development of the score and its appearance. However, many instruments never found their way into orchestras, or they have been used only exceptionally. These include saxophone, basset horn, alto clarinet, tenor oboe, and alto flute, but also widely available instruments such as piano, organ, and guitar. A score rarely indicates the number of players on a given part. As the table below shows, a large orchestra may employ three times as many strings as a small orchestra. A large complement of strings calls for a correspondingly large number of winds. Since all wind parts are solo parts, the number of flutists, for instance, in a given orchestra will indicate whether extra flute players must be hired for performing large works. By adding extra string players for special occasions, a small orchestra can perform music that needs sixteen first and fourteen second violins, twelve violas, ten cellos, and eight basses. This amounts to 8/7/6/5/4 stands with two players each.

The table below shows the makeup of today's typical orchestras that perform classical music. In a large orchestra, not all members necessarily play in all concert or opera performances. Especially in major European cities, an orchestra may be called on to perform so many services that its roster includes an above-average number of players. In cities like Vienna and Stuttgart, the orchestra is large enough that it can be divided into two groups that play on alternate nights. Such an arrangement also requires two concertmasters.

Both small and large orchestras have probably always existed, but the average size has increased steadily since the baroque period. Among the largest orchestras today is the Leipzig Gewandhaus Orchestra,

Instrument	Large orchestra	Midsized orchestra	Small orchestra
First violins	16–24	12–14	8–10
Second violins	14–20	10–12	6–8
Violas	12–16	8–10	4–6
Cellos	10–14	6–8	4–6
Basses	8–10	5–6	3–4
Flutes	5	3–4	3
Oboes	5	3–4	2
Clarinets	5	3–4	3
Bassoons	5	3	2
French horns	8	4–5	4
Trumpets	5	3	3
Trombones	4	3	3
Tubas	1	1	1
Timpani, other percussion	5	4	2–3
Harps	2	1	1
Total	105–129	69–82	49–59

founded more than two hundred years ago. Between 1781 and 1960 its membership grew from 31 to 155. In 1713, the orchestra of the Paris Opéra had only about fifty players; by 1960 it had ninety-five.

The growth of these and other groups was related to musical changes. Among other reasons, woodwind and brass sections were enlarged to produce more varied timbres; to balance their sound, the string section also had to expand. Since 1800, concert halls and other performance venues have become ever larger. The intimate eighteenth-century court theaters gave way to the large opera houses in today's major cities; likewise the drawing rooms of castles were very different from our huge auditoriums. To be audible in these, orchestras must be large. It may well be that early groups, playing on fairly soft instruments, actually sounded louder in an eighteenth-century concert space than do our symphony orchestras in today's large concert halls.

In baroque orchestras we noted the large number of continuo instruments: harpsichord, organ, or both; gamba or cello; often also string bass; one or more bassoons; a bass lute (theorbo) or harp; and for operas a second harpsichord. Usually two to four violins covered each part. In 1730 J. S. Bach stated what he considered desirable for church music: two to three players for first and second violin, four violas, two cellos, one string bass; also two flutes, two oboes, two bassoons, three trumpets, and a pair of kettle drums. But we also have descriptions of performances with far larger forces.

Corelli is said to have performed his music with large numbers of players. Handel festivals in London from 1785 on drew on immense resources. Massed orchestras also took part in public events during the French Revolution. In 1792, an outdoor concert took place on the Paris Champ-de-Mars in which 1200 wind players were heard. Such monster orchestras were, of course, exceptional.

Stylistic changes around 1750 gradually led to the orchestra of the classic period. It included doubled woodwinds and tended to increase the number of players for the upper strings and reduce the cello and bass sections. The Mannheim court orchestra is an example: in 1756 it had ten first and ten second violins but only four cellos and two double basses. Haydn, Mozart, and Beethoven wrote for orchestras such as the one at the Vienna Burgtheater in 1781: six first and six second violins, four violas, three cellos, and three basses. Depending on the occasion, smaller or larger groups might play. Larger ones often were preferred, in which case all the wind parts may have been doubled. Such doubling is rare today and occurs in tutti passages only, if at all, but in general, restrictions on the numbers of players were greater then than today. In 1781 Mozart, full of enthusiasm, described the performance of a symphony of his: forty violins, ten violas, eight cellos, and ten basses participated! For the first performance of Beethoven's Seventh Symphony the orchestra included eighteen first and eighteen second violins, fourteen violas, twelve cellos, and seven basses. The occasion was a concert during the Congress of Vienna in 1814–1815, the meeting that decided Europe's divisions after the Napoleonic Wars. Twenty-four violins participated in the first performance of his Ninth Symphony. Italian opera orchestras were even larger than those in the North. Figure 42 shows the Naples court theater in the royal palace in 1747.   The article "Orchestra" in *The New Grove Dictionary of Music and Musicians* (vol. 13, pp. 679–691) gives much additional information, including many seating plans and tables indicating numbers of players at various times and places.

Today, most symphonies and operas are performed with orchestras of typical nineteenth-century proportions. Haydn's and Mozart's symphonies (except Mozart's last three), however, are played by a smaller ensemble, even if more players are available. Most conductors want eight to ten players each for first and second violin parts—the small orchestra listed in the third column of the table above.

Seating plans

In baroque orchestras the continuo group formed the nucleus, seated center stage, with the other players grouped around it. Standardized seating arrangements such as we have today did not yet exist in the early eighteenth century. In one frequently found plan the strings and winds sat on the left and right sides of the continuo group. This manner of separating them was observed in many opera orchestras well into the nineteenth century. In 1775, Johann Friedrich Reichardt in Berlin introduced the seating plan that generally prevailed, at least in Germany, until ca. 1945. First and second violins sit opposite each other, at the conductor's left and right. Cellos are in front of the conductor, basses to their left, violas to their right. Woodwinds sit behind the strings; brass and timpani behind them. Reichardt's plan is sometimes called traditional or classic (see figures 43 and 44a). In smaller orchestras woodwinds and brass sections are closer to each other.

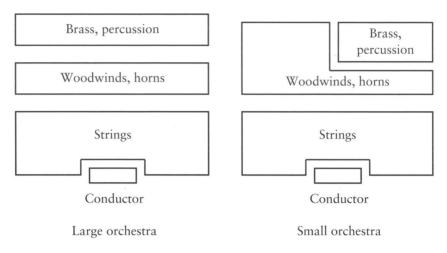

43. Seating plans (strings and winds) for large and small orchestras

After World War II, most German orchestras adopted the "American" seating plan, with first violins and cellos on the conductor's left and right, respectively (see figure 44b). Leopold Stokowski was the first to use this plan; it corresponds to a standard string quartet seating. Wilhelm Furtwängler, while conductor of the Berlin Philharmonic, introduced a variation of the American seating in which violas and cellos have exchanged places (see figure 44c). Other orchestras have adopted this layout.

Opera orchestras sit in the usually very cramped quarters of the pit in front of the stage. Figure 45 shows cross sections of a normal orchestra pit and of the unusual one in Bayreuth, constructed according to Wagner's specifications. As the diagram shows, the Bayreuth orchestra is invisible to the audience, whereas in other opera houses the players can be seen from balcony and gallery seats. Opera orchestras have no standard seating plan.

a) Traditional seating

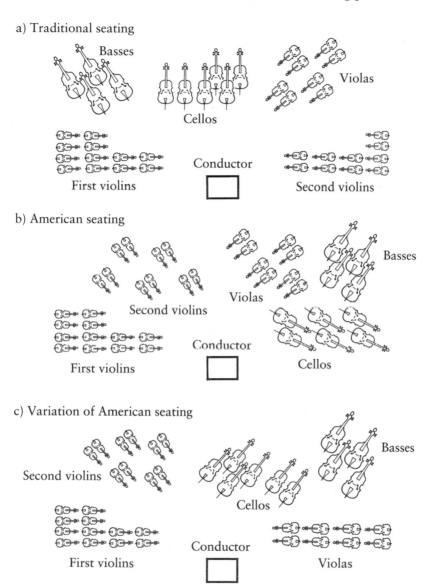

b) American seating

c) Variation of American seating

44. Various seating plans for string players

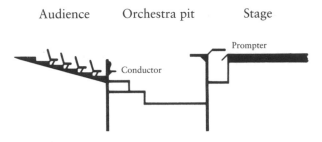

Traditional orchestra pit

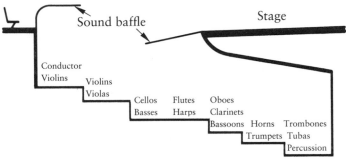

Orchestra pit at Bayreuth Festspielhaus

45. Orchestra pits in opera houses

Spatial effects

Each of the seating plans described above has advantages and disadvantages. In the traditional plan, first and second violins are far apart. This makes echo passages very effective but makes precise ensemble playing difficult. The plan is good for the cellos because their sound projects well to the audience. With the American seating, echo, or "back and forth" effects between first and second violins are likely to be lost because of the proximity of the two sections, but better ensemble between them and between second violins and violas may result. Cellos are heard to better advantage in Furtwängler's plan, but good ensemble between second violins and violas is more difficult to obtain.

In general the American plan makes for precise ensemble playing and the traditional plan provides good separation of sound.

Examining scores helps in the search for the right seating plan. Much of the standard orchestra repertory was written during a period when the traditional seating plan was the norm. Did this affect composers in their writing? Quite a few scores suggest it, especially in the handling of violin parts. Thus Beethoven wrote the following passage for his Fourth Symphony, while the other instruments have rests:

46. Creation of spatial effect in orchestral writing (Beethoven, Fourth Symphony)

It would seem to be easier for the orchestra to play the passage this way:

Of course, this second arrangement would be simpler and easier, but Beethoven evidently had a spatial effect in mind, wanting to toss the phrase back and forth. Such an effect can only be achieved with the traditional seating plan. Tchaikovsky's Sixth Symphony is another good example of a composition designed around the traditional seating. The last movement's principal theme is heard in two versions that are identical except for the spatial effects. Also remember that upon hearing tones of similar timbre our ears tend to combine and interpret the highest ones as a melody, as shown in figure 47a. The melody wanders back and forth between first and second violins—it "swings" through space. This wandering melody begins the last movement. Later, the melody returns in the version shown in figure 47b: it no longer moves through space but remains on the ground. Surely Tchaikovsky created these effects intentionally; they seem to require the traditional seating plan. Viola and cello parts are similarly intertwined.

The conductor

In any kind of ensemble it is a challenge to have everyone play exactly together and to achieve accurate intonation and dynamic balance. Constant listening and adjusting are required. In this the acoustics of the hall or recording studio play an important role. The ceiling above the orchestra podium must reflect the individual instruments' sound effectively.

To achieve the goals of clean intonation, rhythmic precision, and dynamic balance, a conductor is needed, because individual players from their places within the group cannot judge and control the overall effect that reaches the audience. It is also nearly impossible to decide on the total interpretive concept in a democratic way; in the long run, one artist must be responsible. Considering how complex an apparatus a large orchestra is, the precision timing often achieved is remarkable. Discrepancies in attacks seldom exceed one-twentieth to one-thirtieth of a second. Actually, such minor discrepancies help form the characteristic orchestral sound, reinforcing the impression of fullness, of magnitude received by the listener. They are part of the fascination of orchestral music.

Through the ages, large groups of musicians, whether instrumental or choral, have relied on some kind of direction. The point at which a group requires a director cannot be stated with precision. It depends not only on the number of musicians but also on their abilities and on the difficulty of the music. Chamber music, unlike orchestral music, normally does not call for a conductor, but some complex works, such

47. Creation of spatial effect in violin parts (Tchaikovsky, Sixth Symphony)

as Stravinsky's *L'histoire du soldat* for seven instruments, often are conducted.

Just like the notation of music, the ways of directing an orchestra or similar group have changed over time. Some earlier ways of directing may seem strange if not ludicrous, just as some old kinds of notation are puzzling. Yet every style period used a type of direction appropriate for it. Also, various ways of conducting an orchestra correspond to the style of the music and the demands it makes on the players. Today, the professional conductor occupies a central place in concert life; it is a position that evolved only gradually in the nineteenth century, the age when the orchestra also acquired its current basic makeup. The nineteenth century also produced most of the repertory heard today.

During the sixteenth and seventeenth centuries, the person in charge of music at court was called *Kapellmeister* in German, *maestro di capella* in Italian. In German towns, leaders of orchestras and choirs usually were employed by the town or by church authorities and were called director of music, sometimes cantor. When the word *Kapelle* lost its earlier meaning—the music establishment at court—the title *Kapellmeister* was replaced by *Dirigent*, conductor in English.

In renaissance musical practice, the leader of an ensemble merely marked the basic beat or pulse, the *tactus*, by raising and lowering his hand. He often also participated in the performance. Later, during the seventeenth and eighteenth centuries, the leader directed from the harpsichord, on which he played the continuo. J. M. Gesner, a chronicler writing in 1738, paints a lively picture of how J. S. Bach officiated as a conductor:

> He keeps close track of thirty to forty musicians, by waving a hand or by marking time with his foot. He cautions one of his charges by shaking a finger at him; he will give the correct pitch, in a high, middle, or low register, to those who need help. Though the musicians produce a great din, he immediately notices when anything is about to go wrong. He has an inborn sense of rhythm, an extremely keen ear for harmony, and he will sing all voice parts in spite of the limited range of his own voice.

Aside from the maestro at the harpsichord, Bach's age also knew the leader who conducted singers or players by marking time with a scroll of sheet music or with a stick (see figure 48). Our modern patterns of beating time go back to seventeenth- and early eighteenth-century France. There, conductors also had the unfortunate habit of audibly beating time, on the floor, with a large baton. According to an often-told story, Jean-Baptiste Lully, composer at the court of Louis XIV, accidentally hit his foot with the baton, resulting in a wound and infection that led to his death. Curiously enough, the accident happened during a concert celebrating the king's recovery from a serious illness.

18. Niccolò Jommelli, conducting with a scroll of music paper (engraving, ca. 1750)

For eighteenth-century opera performances, a kind of double direction was customary. The maestro at the harpsichord was aided by the concertmaster who, as leader of the first violins, not only played his part but also gave cues to other musicians. For this he would write cues in his own part. Occasionally he would do some informal conducting with his bow. Double direction disappeared with the baroque age. After 1800, conductors as we think of them arrived on the scene, standing on a podium and using a short, slender baton that still is their trademark today. Nevertheless, even in the mid-nineteenth century some groups were conducted by the concertmaster.

Most early conductors in our sense also were composers: Spontini, Spohr, Weber, and Mendelssohn. Only in the later nineteenth century did the two professions become separated. Still some were opposed to the professional conductor. Schumann believed that an orchestra was, or should be, a republic, without a "higher-up who made the decisions."

Conducting technique

Conductors have two basic tasks. They must ensure precise ensemble playing, for which purpose they use certain patterns of beating time. Furthermore, their gestures must convey to the players the concepts of tempo, dynamics, balance, timbre, and phrasing. Time beating, gestures, facial expression, even "body language"—conductors rely on all these to communicate their intentions to the players.

Beating time usually is done with the right hand; it holds the baton, which amplifies and clarifies the beat patterns. These motions must be elastic, not rigid. Figure 49 shows the traditional beat patterns. Sometimes they are reinforced by corresponding, symmetrical motions in the left hand.

By the way they are executed, these time-beating motions can also signal interpretive commands. The right or left hand may direct a section of the orchestra to play louder or softer. Such directions can also be communicated by the conductor's facial expression or body position, but they are chiefly given with the left hand, which therefore must move independently of the right hand, as the situation requires. Gradually raising the left hand may call for a crescendo, lowering it for a decrescendo. Aside from tempo and dynamics, conductors must communicate their intentions about phrasing, clarifying how the music "hangs together," indicating meaningful subdivisions of longer lines. But no matter how perfect a conductor's technique, his or her personality as perceived by the players will markedly affect the precision and interpretation, and hence the success of a performance.

When only the down beat in every bar is to be indicated (regardless of the time signature), the "One" is emphasized by a strong, elastic downward motion of the hand(s). This pattern is used for a rapid tempo.

This is the pattern for all duple meters (2/2 and 2/4) and for rapid 4/4 and 6/8 time when only beats one and three (or one and four) are given.

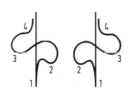

In triple time (3/4, 3/8, 9/8), the upward "bounce" is interrupted twice. If the tempo is very fast, the conductor may give only the first beat.

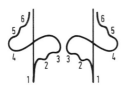

Normal pattern for conducting 4/4 time.

Six-eight (6/8) time also has a secondary accent, on beat four. As in 4/4 time, it is indicated by a distinct motion to the outside.

49. Conducting patterns, or beat patterns, for various time signatures

Gustav Mahler, based on a drawing by Hans Böhler

8 Instrumentation and Score Reading: Suggestions for Further Reading

The art and science of instrumentation deals with the assigning of tones, motives, themes, and so on, to specific instruments. It therefore determines the tone colors, the timbres of a composition as documented in the score, but also the volume of sound. Instrumentation is an essential part of the composition—it is not like a copper engraving that later is colored. To an extent, instrumentation can be taught: strengths and limitations of each instrument, their ranges, and so forth. But beyond that it is an art, for which reason it is one of the most interesting aspects of a score.

Much has been written on the art of instrumentation. Perhaps the most influential study is by Hector Berlioz. He developed the art of instrumentation to a point not reached before and explained it in his *Grand traité d'instrumentation et d'orchestration modernes* (Paris, 1844, Engl. tran. London, 1850, 1856; there are many later editions). Berlioz's skill is evident in his works of program music in which he used specific instruments to characterize persons, situations, and moods. Today his treatise is widely consulted in the revised, updated edition by Richard Strauss (1st ed. Leipzig, 1905; Engl. tran. New York, 1948). That edition includes many music examples by Wagner and Strauss himself. All orchestra instruments are discussed, including some rarely heard in an orchestra, such as guitar, heckelphone, and the various saxophones.

To play an orchestral score on the piano requires considerable skill and practice. It is an important part of a conductor's training and goes far beyond the ability to follow a score. The two works listed below (there are others) are intended for students of conducting, but readers may find them interesting, just to understand what skills are involved and how one acquires them. Two main challenges in playing a full orchestral score come from transposing instruments and from clefs other than the familiar treble and bass clefs. Both these titles are available in many U.S. libraries.

Martin Bernstein, *Score Reading: A Series of Graded Excerpts* (New York, 1947). Includes exercises with transposing instruments and tables giving pitch names and instrument names in four languages. Music examples range from J. S. Bach to Stravinsky.

Egon Bölsche, *Schule des Partiturspiels* (School of playing from a score; Leipzig, 1952). Chiefly devoted to exercises using many old clefs.

The two books cited below are intended for non-professionals who wish to improve their skills at reading, following, and understanding a composition. They are shorter, basic introductions to the subject.

Gordon Jacob, *How to Read a Score* (London, 1944, 1956). Sixty-seven pages. Contains no music examples, but provides a useful list of orchestral works prominently featuring various instruments. Chapter 6, "Aural Imagination," deals with the extent to which the average listener can "hear" a score while reading it. Chapter 5 outlines some special effects possible on string, woodwind, brass, and percussion instruments.

Philip Cranmer, *How to Follow a Score* (London, 1981). Sixty pages. A very concise introduction. The music examples are taken from orchestral scores published by Eulenburg, Ltd., London.

MICHAEL DICKREITER was born in Konstanz, Germany, in 1942. He earned a Tonmeister (sound engineer) diploma from Detmold Music Academy and a Ph.D. from Heidelberg University with a dissertation on the music theories of Johannes Kepler. He is an instructor at the School for Radio Technique in Nuremberg, which is operated by the German State Broadcasting System. He is the author of several books on sound recording techniques, acoustics, and musical instruments.

REINHARD G. PAULY, translator, is professor emeritus at Lewis and Clark College, where he was director of the School of Music. He served as general editor of Amadeus Press for the first ten years of the press's existence. A native of Germany, he holds degrees from Columbia and Yale universities, and for many years played both violin and viola in professional orchestras.